MICROSOFT 365 EXCEL TIPS, TRICKS AND TECHNIQUES

Elevare
LEARNING
ACADEMY

PROJECT TEAM

Greg Williams
Andrew Lumsdaine

VERSION

1.0

TRADEMARKS

Microsoft, Microsoft Windows, Microsoft 365, and Microsoft Excel are registered trademarks of the Microsoft Corporation. All other brand and product names are trademarks or registered trademarks of their respective companies.

DISCLAIMER

We make sincere effort to ensure the accuracy of the material described herein, however Elevare Learning Academy makes no warranty, express or implied, with respect to the quality, correctness, reliability, currentness, accuracy, or freedom from error of this document or the products it describes. Elevare Learning Academy makes no representation or warranty with respect to the contents hereof and specifically disclaims any implied warranties of fitness for any particular purpose.

Elevare Learning Academy disclaims all liability for any direct, indirect, incidental or consequential, special or exemplary damages resulting from the use of the information in this document. Mention of any product does not constitute an endorsement by Elevare Learning Academy of that product. Data used in examples and sample data files is intended to be fictional. Any resemblance to real persons or companies is entirely coincidental.

The features and instructions described in this manual are accurate for Excel for Microsoft 365, current as of September 2025. Future updates to Excel may result in changes to menus, commands, or functionality.

Download the Companion Resources

To help you apply the techniques in this book more easily, we've provided a complete set of sample files and ready-to-use macro code. You can download these companion resources at:

www.elevarelearning.com.au/excel-ttt-resources

These files give you immediate access to practical examples and code that align directly with the book's content.

TABLE OF CONTENTS

About This Book

Have you ever watched someone use Excel and thought *"How did they do that?"* or *"Why does it take me twice as long to complete the same task?"*

Excel is filled with shortcuts and features that are often overlooked. Discovering them is the key to working faster and more effectively.

This *Excel Tips, Tricks & Techniques* book contains over 200 practical ideas to help you boost efficiency and uncover many of Excel's hidden tools. It aims to answer those familiar questions such as *"I wonder if Excel can..."* or *"There must be a quicker way to..."* and provide solutions you can use immediately.

A complete list of keyboard commands is included along with a selection of ready-to-use macros that can automate tasks once thought impossible.

The tips are grouped into chapters such as *Navigating and Selecting*, *Printing*, and *Formulas and Functions*. There is no need to read in order. Simply choose a chapter, select a technique, and try it out. Screenshots and sample data are included throughout to make it easy to follow along, or you can create your own practice spreadsheets.

Although written with Microsoft 365 Excel in mind, most of these tips will also work in other versions.

Enjoy exploring these techniques and the time, confidence, and productivity they will add to your everyday work with this powerful software.

Conventions

This book follows a consistent set of conventions.

- Excel files are referred to as **workbooks**. A workbook may contain several sheets, referred to as **worksheets**.

- The Ribbon is the strip at the top of Excel that organises all the main commands and tools. It consists of a series of tabs (e.g. Home, Insert, Page Layout, Formulas, Data, etc.). Commands on each tab of the Ribbon are grouped into categories. When describing how to select commands from the Ribbon, the tab, group and command are all shown in bold, for example, "Select the **Data** tab and from the **Forecast** group click on the **What-If Analysis** button and then select **Goal Seek**."

- When referring to the name of a dialog box, the name shown in the title bar of the dialog box will appear in quotation marks, for example, "The "Paste Special" dialog box will be displayed".

- Buttons and tabs in dialog boxes that are clicked on are shown in bold and preceded with the word "click", for example, "Click the **Add** button".

- Commands that are entered from the keyboard are represented in uppercase and in bold, for example, "Press **CTRL+S** to save the workbook".

- When describing commands that are enabled/disabled via a check box, e.g.:

☑ Show Mini Toolbar on selection

the command "enable" means to turn the feature on (ie: a tick/check appears in the box) and the command "disable" means to turn the feature off (ie: no tick/check appears in the box). For example, "Disable **Show Mini Toolbar on selection** option".

- Cross references to other tips, tricks, or techniques appear in brackets, with the item name in italics and quotation marks, for example, "(refer to "*Selecting Non-Continuous Cells*" for further information)".

- Menus that are displayed as a result of right-clicking are referred to as **shortcut menus**, as shown below.

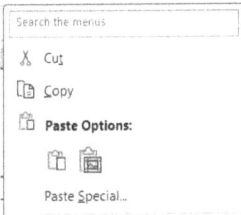

- Macro commands that you need to enter are shown in a different typeface, as shown below.

```
Sub StuffTogether()
Dim FirstCol As Integer, FirstRow As Integer
```

NAVIGATING AND SELECTING

Moving Around Tabbed Dialog Boxes with the Keyboard

You can move from one tab to another in any of Excel's multi-page dialog boxes by pressing **CTRL+TAB** or **CTRL+PGDN** on the keyboard.

Number   Alignment   Font   Border   Fill   Protection

Pressing **CTRL+SHIFT+TAB** or **CTRL+PGUP** will move back through the tabs in the opposite direction.

Moving Quickly Across the Worksheet

You may have used the **PGUP** and **PGDN** keys to quickly move up and down one screen at a time. Excel also has keystrokes that allow you to move quickly across the worksheet, one screen at a time. Pressing **ALT+PGDN** will move one screen to the right and **ALT+PGUP** will move one screen to the left.

Moving and Selecting Ranges Quickly

You can move to the boundaries of a range (the group of cells bounded by blank cells in any direction) quickly by double-clicking the different borders of the active cell pointer.

Ensure that the mouse pointer displays as the arrow shaped pointer ( ) before double-clicking on the border of a cell.

For example;
- double-clicking the bottom cell border will take you to the bottom cell in the range.
- double-clicking the right border will take you to the furthest cell right in the range.
- double-clicking the top border will take you to the top cell in the range.
- double-clicking the left border will take you to the furthest cell left in the range.

This feature is a great way of moving around ranges that are too large to fit on the screen.

Note: You can use this technique with the **SHIFT** key to select cells, for example, holding down **SHIFT** and double-clicking the bottom cell border will select from the current cell to the last cell downwards in the range.

Checking a Column or a Row for Data Before Deleting

Removing entire rows or columns in Excel carries a risk, as data may exist outside the visible area of your worksheet. To avoid accidental loss, use the following technique to check for hidden data before deleting.

Press the **END** key and then press one of the directional keys (eg: **END** then the **DOWN ARROW**). The cell pointer will move to the next cell in that direction that contains data. If there aren't any cells containing data in that column or row, you will be taken to the last column (XFD) or row (1048576) of the spreadsheet.

This technique can also be useful for moving about in large spreadsheets. A useful variation of this command is to use **END** and then **HOME** to move to the last active cell of the spreadsheet.

Note: Pressing **CTRL** and any of the arrow keys (at the same time) is the equivalent of using the technique with the **END** key described above.

You can use the **SHIFT** key with the **END / ARROW KEY** combination described above to select cells, ie: to select from the current cell to the end of a range of cells, hold down **SHIFT** whilst pressing **END** and then the **DOWN ARROW**.

The End of the Worksheet

In a similar way to the **CTRL+HOME** keystroke (which moves the cell pointer to the start of the spreadsheet), the keystroke **CTRL+END** can be used to move the cell pointer to the last cell of the spreadsheet containing data (the intersection of the right-most column and the bottom-most row).

However, if information is deleted from the spreadsheet, the **CTRL+END** keystroke may continue to go to the original "end" of the spreadsheet, even though the cell is now empty.

One reason for this situation is that although the data has been deleted from cells at the end of the spreadsheet, the cell formats remain. To remove cell contents as well as cell formatting, select the cells you want to clear and use the **Clear All** command from the **Home** tab on the Ribbon.

You should also save the worksheet after deleting cells, columns or rows so that Excel can recalculate the "end" cell location.

Viewing the Active Cell

Sometimes when you are scrolling through a spreadsheet (ie: using the scrollbars not the keyboard), you lose sight of where the cell pointer is because you have scrolled out of the active part of the screen.

You can quickly go back to the active cell by pressing **CTRL+BACKSPACE** on the keyboard.

Go To

In addition to being able to type in a cell reference, the "Go To" dialog box displays the last four locations that you have been to using this feature, along with the range names that exist on the current sheet.

To activate the "Go To" dialog box, select the **Home** tab on the Ribbon, and in the **Editing** group, click the **Find & Select** button and select **Go To** from the drop-down menu.

Note: There are two keyboard shortcuts for the Go To command, **F5** and **CTRL+G**.

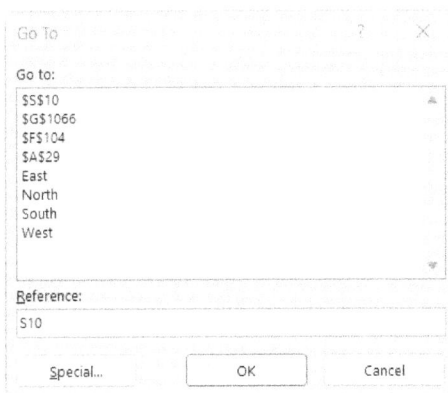

Go To	?	×

Go to:

$S$10	
$G$1066	
$F$104	
$A$29	
East	
North	
South	
West	

Reference:

S10

Special...	OK	Cancel

Special Go To Features

You may have used the Go To feature (refer to "*Go To*") to move the cell pointer to a particular cell reference or range name. In addition to this feature, the Go To command has a series of features that are available by clicking on the **Special** button, located at the bottom of the dialog box.

These special features include the ability to select cells containing formulas, conditional formats and validation rules.

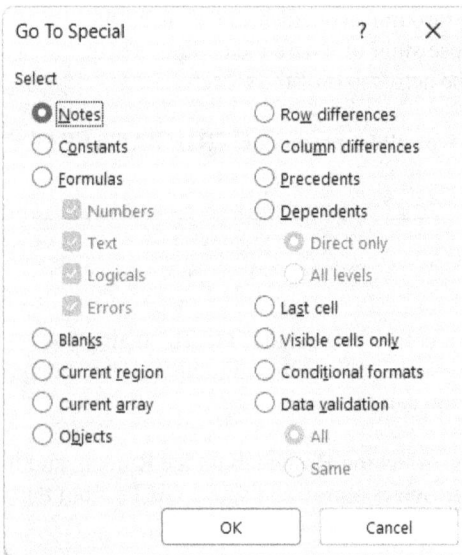

Go To Special	? ✕
Select	
⦿ Notes	◯ Row differences
◯ Constants	◯ Column differences
◯ Formulas	◯ Precedents
☑ Numbers	◯ Dependents
☑ Text	◉ Direct only
☑ Logicals	◯ All levels
☑ Errors	◯ Last cell
◯ Blanks	◯ Visible cells only
◯ Current region	◯ Conditional formats
◯ Current array	◯ Data validation
◯ Objects	◉ All
	◯ Same
OK	Cancel

Navigating Between Multiple Sheets Quickly

Rather than having to scroll through the sheet tabs to locate a worksheet that you require, you can right-click over the sheet tab navigation buttons ‹ › .

A list of the sheet tab names is displayed. You can then double-click on a sheet tab name to move quickly to that sheet.

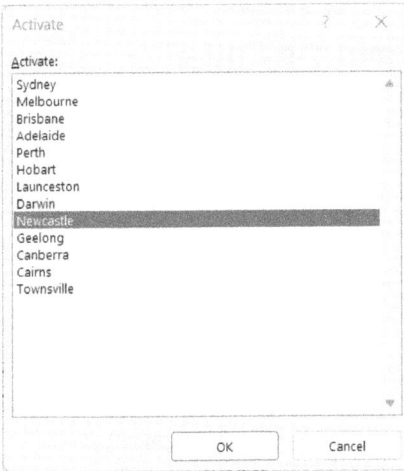

Note: You can also use the keyboard commands **CTRL+PGDN** and **CTRL+PGUP** to move between sheets in a workbook.

Using the Name Box to Go To a Specific Cell

You can use the "Name Box" (located under the Ribbon) to go to a specific cell reference. Simply click in the box, type in the cell reference and press **ENTER**.

To move quickly to a named area of the spreadsheet, click on the drop-down arrow located next to the Name Box. A list of defined range names will be displayed. Clicking on a range name will take the cell pointer to that area of the spreadsheet.

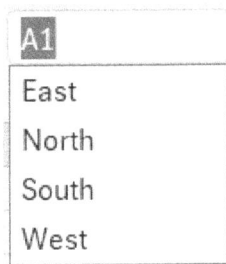

Selecting Columns, Rows and the Entire Worksheet

To select an entire column, click on the column heading with the mouse, or press **CTRL+spacebar** on the keyboard to select the column containing the cell pointer.

To select an entire row, click on the row heading with the mouse, or press **SHIFT+spacebar** on the keyboard to select the row containing the cell pointer.

To select the entire sheet, click on the blank square located above row 1 and to the left of column A, or press **CTRL+A** (or **CTRL+SHIFT+spacebar**) on the keyboard.

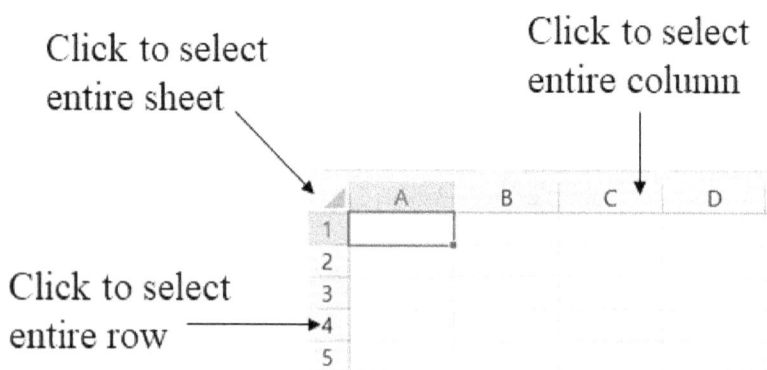

Selecting Non-Continuous Cells

Excel allows you to select ranges that are non-continuous (ie: not located together). This is useful when you want to use the same command on several cells that are located in different areas of the worksheet.

1) Select the first cell(s) that you want included in the range.
2) Hold down the **CTRL** key.
3) Select the next cell(s) that you want included in the range.

As long as you continue to hold down the **CTRL** key, additional cells will be added to the selection. Any feature that is applied will effect all of the selected cells.

Selecting the Current Range

You can select the current active area (range) by pressing **CTRL+SHIFT+8** or **CTRL+ASTERISK** (on the numeric keypad). The current active area is the rectangular cell range around the active cell, bounded by any combination of blank rows and blank columns.

Selecting Ranges with the Shift Key

The **SHIFT** key, when used in conjunction with Excel's navigation keys, can be used to select ranges of any size. For example, pressing **SHIFT+Right Arrow** will select cells to the right, **SHIFT+PGDN** will select cells in a downwards direction one screen at a time, **SHIFT+ALT+PGDN** will select cells to the right one screen at a time.

A particularly useful variation is **SHIFT+CTRL+END**, which selects from the current cell to the last used cell in the worksheet.

You can also select multiple sheets from the keyboard by pressing **SHIFT+CTRL+PGUP** and **SHIFT+CTRL+PGDN**.

Selecting Ranges with the Extend Feature

Another method of selecting cells with the keyboard involves using the **F8** (Extend) key. After pressing **F8**, all keyboard movement commands (eg: using arrow keys etc.) become selections.

For example, pressing **F8** and then hitting the down arrow three times will select the current cell and the next three cells down the screen. Pressing **F8** and then **CTRL+END** will select from the current cell to the end of the spreadsheet data. A message will be displayed on the status bar whilst in "extend mode", as shown below.

Extend Selection

Once the required cells have been selected, press **F8** again to turn off the extend feature.

Note: You can also use the keyboard to select non-continuous ranges (refer to "*Selecting Non-Continuous Cells*" for information on using the mouse to select non-continuous ranges). Use the **F8** key as described above to select the first cell(s) of the range. Then press **SHIFT+F8** to activate the "Add" feature. Move the cell pointer to the start of the next area you want to select using the arrow keys. The original area should remain selected whilst you move the cell pointer to the start of the new location. Press **F8** and start selecting the next group of cells. Continue to use the **SHIFT+F8** and **F8** keys until the areas you require have been selected.

Selecting a Large Range Without Dragging

If you have ever had to select a large area of a spreadsheet, you may have noticed that Excel tends to "run away" as you start to scroll off the screen. The following steps describe a technique for selecting a large group of cells without having to perform the traditional "click and drag" routine.

1) Click in the cell at the top left of the area you want to select.
2) If necessary, use the scroll bar to scroll through the spreadsheet so that the bottom right cell of the area you want to select is visible.
3) Hold down the **SHIFT** key on the keyboard.
4) Click once in the bottom right cell of the area you want to select.

The area between the two cells that you clicked on will be selected.

Selecting a Range with Go To

The following technique lets you select a large range without using the mouse, as long as you know the address of the bottom-right cell.

1) Click in the cell at the top left of the area you want to select.
2) Press **F5** to display the "Go To" dialog box.
3) Type in the cell reference that represents the bottom right of the range you want to select.
4) Hold down the **SHIFT** key whilst clicking on **OK**.

Zoom to Selection

Most people use the Zoom control to change the magnification of the whole worksheet, but you can also zoom in on just the cells you've selected.

Highlight the range you want to enlarge, then select the **View** tab on the Ribbon and from the **Zoom** group, click **Zoom to Selection**. Excel automatically adjusts the zoom level so your selection fills the window as much as possible.

This is a quick way to focus on the part of your sheet you're working on, without constant scrolling or guessing the zoom percentage.

Scroll Super Fast

Hold down the **SHIFT** key while dragging the vertical or horizontal scroll bar to move quickly through your worksheet. The scroll bar shrinks in size, and a tooltip shows the row or column number as you zip along. Keep **SHIFT** held down as you scroll until you reach the spot in the worksheet that you want.

AUTOFILL

Using the Fill Handle

If a cell contains a number, date, or time period that Excel recognises as part of a sequence, you can use the Fill Handle, the small square in the lower-right corner of the cell, to automatically continue the pattern. For example, if you enter "January" in a cell, dragging the Fill Handle across a row or down a column will fill the adjacent cells with "February", "March", and so on.

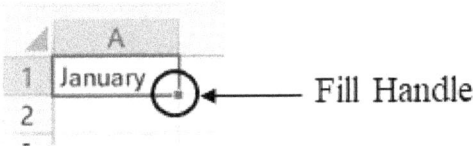

Fill Handle

You can drag the Fill Handle downward to extend a series in a column or to the right to extend it across a row. Dragging diagonally is not possible, so you need to complete one direction first, release the mouse, and then drag again in the other direction. As you drag, Excel shows a screen tip with the value that will appear in each cell, giving you instant feedback before you release the mouse.

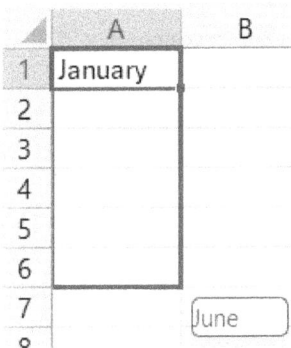

The following spreadsheet shows some examples of the AutoFill feature.

	A	B	C	D	E	F	G	H	I
1	January	Monday	Jan	Mon	Qtr 1	Week 1	Product 1	10/09/2025	9:00 AM
2	February	Tuesday	Feb	Tue	Qtr 2	Week 2	Product 2	11/09/2025	10:00 AM
3	March	Wednesday	Mar	Wed	Qtr 3	Week 3	Product 3	12/09/2025	11:00 AM
4	April	Thursday	Apr	Thu	Qtr 4	Week 4	Product 4	13/09/2025	12:00 PM
5	May	Friday	May	Fri	Qtr 1	Week 5	Product 5	14/09/2025	1:00 PM
6	June	Saturday	Jun	Sat	Qtr 2	Week 6	Product 6	15/09/2025	2:00 PM
7	July	Sunday	Jul	Sun	Qtr 3	Week 7	Product 7	16/09/2025	3:00 PM
8	August	Monday	Aug	Mon	Qtr 4	Week 8	Product 8	17/09/2025	4:00 PM
9	September	Tuesday	Sep	Tue	Qtr 1	Week 9	Product 9	18/09/2025	5:00 PM
10	October	Wednesday	Oct	Wed	Qtr 2	Week 10	Product 10	19/09/2025	6:00 PM
11	November	Thursday	Nov	Thu	Qtr 3	Week 11	Product 11	20/09/2025	7:00 PM
12	December	Friday	Dec	Fri	Qtr 4	Week 12	Product 12	21/09/2025	8:00 PM

AutoFill Options Button

After using AutoFill, an AutoFill Options button appears next to the filled area. Clicking this button lets you choose how the cells are completed:

- **Copy Cells** – repeats the original value
- **Fill Series** – continues a recognised pattern
- **Fill Formatting Only** – applies the formatting without changing the values
- **Fill Without Formatting** – extends the values but leaves out the formatting.

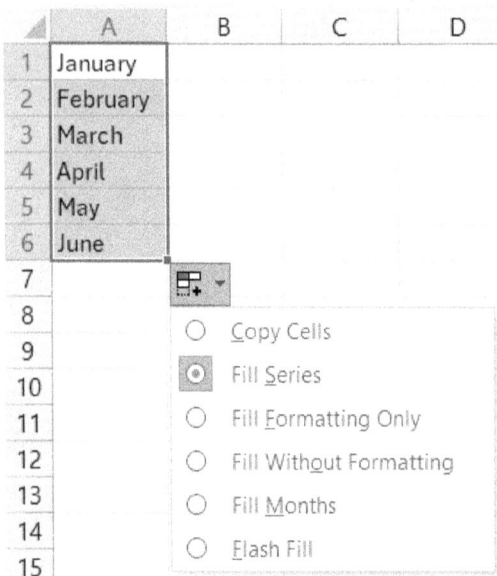

If you have filled a series of dates, additional options, such as **Fill Weekdays** are available.

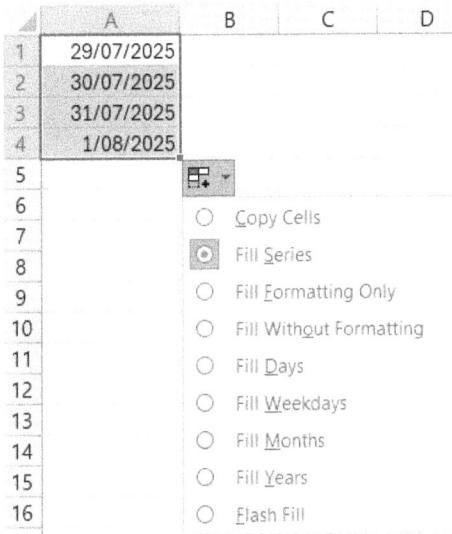

	A	B	C	D
1	29/07/2025			
2	30/07/2025			
3	31/07/2025			
4	1/08/2025			
5				
6		○ Copy Cells		
7		◉ Fill Series		
8				
9		○ Fill Formatting Only		
10		○ Fill Without Formatting		
11		○ Fill Days		
12		○ Fill Weekdays		
13				
14		○ Fill Months		
15		○ Fill Years		
16		○ Flash Fill		

AutoFilling Numbers

You may have used the fill handle to complete sequences of months, days, quarters, weeks, etc. (refer to "*Using the Fill Handle*"). However, when you try and AutoFill numbers (eg: 1999, 2000), Excel simply copies the first number as you fill. There are two ways to correct this.

1) Type in the first number and hold down the **CTRL** key as you fill.

OR

2) Enter the first two numbers in the sequence, select both and then fill.

The second method allows you to fill numbers, dates and months in different sequences (eg: every four years, every fortnight, etc.) as shown below.

	A	B	C	D
1	1999	1999	Jan	1/08/2025
2	2000	2003	Apr	8/08/2025
3	2001	2007	Jul	15/08/2025
4	2002	2011	Oct	22/08/2025
5	2003	2015	Jan	29/08/2025
6	2004	2019	Apr	5/09/2025
7	2005	2023	Jul	12/09/2025
8	2006	2027	Oct	19/09/2025

Creating a Custom AutoFill Series

In addition to the standard AutoFill sequences such as years, months, and days, Excel also lets you create custom fill lists. These are especially useful for entering repetitive sets of data, such as branch locations, sales representatives, or product names.

1) Select the **File** tab on the Ribbon and then select the **Options** command.

2) Select the **Advanced** category and in the **General** section, click on the **Edit Custom Lists** button.

3) Click on the **Add** button. The cursor should start flashing in the "List entries" column.

4) Type in the entries for the custom list. They can either be separated by a comma or by pressing **ENTER** after each entry.

| Custom Lists | | ? ✕ |

Custom Lists

Custom lists: List entries:

NEW LIST	General	Add
Mon, Tue, Wed, Thu, Fri, Sat, Sun	Lieutenant General	
Monday, Tuesday, Wednesday, Thu	Major General	Delete
Jan, Feb, Mar, Apr, May, Jun, Jul, Au	Brigadier	
January, February, March, April, Ma	Colonel	
	Lieutenant Colonel	
	Major	
	Captain	
	Lieutenant	
	Second Lieutenant	

Press Enter to separate list entries.
Import list from cells: ⬆ Import

OK   Cancel

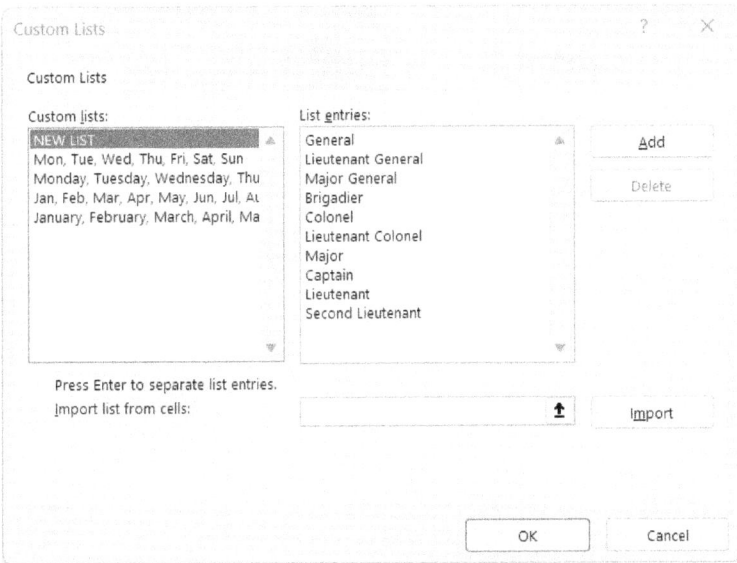

5) Click **OK** to complete the list entry and **OK** to return to the spreadsheet.

6) To use the list, type any one of the list items in a cell and then use the fill handle to fill the other entries, either down or across the screen.

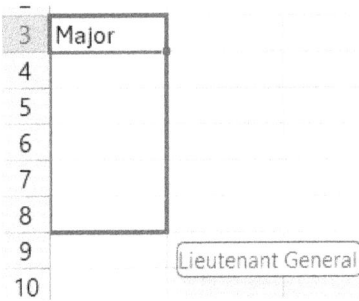

3	Major
4	
5	
6	
7	
8	
9	Lieutenant General
10	

Note: You can also create a custom list from data that exists in the spreadsheet. Highlight the list of values that you want to use, select the **File ➔ Options** command, select the **Advanced** category and in the **General** section, click on the **Edit Custom Lists** button, then click the **Import** button.

Using the Right Mouse Button with AutoFill

There are a variety of different AutoFill options available if you drag the fill handle using the right mouse button.

For example, if you have two values selected and then use the right mouse button to drag the fill handle, a different menu appears, including options for creating a "Growth Trend".

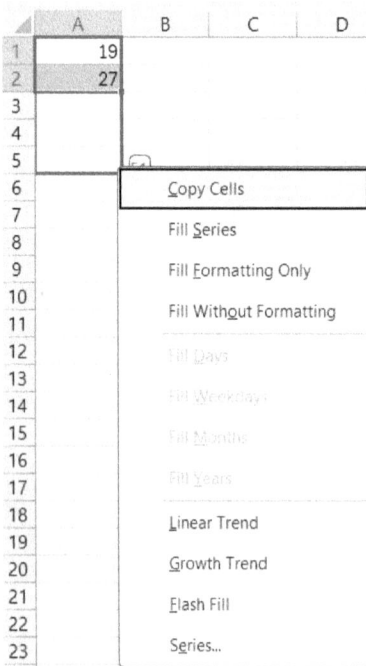

Using the Fill Handle to Insert Cells, Rows or Columns

Using the **SHIFT** key with the Fill Handle allows you to insert cells, rows or columns.

For example, with the cell pointer positioned in cell A4 as shown below, holding down **SHIFT** and dragging the Fill Handle to cell A6 will insert two new cells underneath A4 (existing data in the column is pushed down).

Note that the mouse pointer changes shape to the column/row sizing pointer when you hold down the **SHIFT** key over the Fill Handle.

	A	B	C
1	**Product**	**Unit Price**	**Qty Sold**
2	DriftBrew	$2.19	59,915
3	Voltéa	$3.65	110,100
4	BloomSip	$1.86	109,353
5	Frostroot	$5.33	77,257
6	Solara	$1.94	83,959
7	Moss & Mint	$3.01	97,480

If an entire row is selected as shown below, holding down **SHIFT** whilst dragging the Fill Handle will insert entire rows underneath row 4. When an entire row is selected, the Fill Handle moves to the left of the active cell, next to the row numbers. A similar situation occurs when an entire column is selected.

Fill Handle

	A	B	C	D
1	Product	Unit Price	Qty Sold	
2	DriftBrew	$2.19	59,915	
3	Voltéa	$3.65	110,100	
4	BloomSip	$1.86	109,353	
5	Frostroot	$5.33	77,257	
6	Solara	$1.94	83,959	
7	Moss & Mint	$3.01	97,480	

	A	B	C
1	Product	Unit Price	Qty Sold
2	DriftBrew	$2.19	59,915
3	Voltéa	$3.65	110,100
4	BloomSip	$1.86	109,353
5	Frostroot	$5.33	77,257
6	Solara	$1.94	83,959
7	Moss & Mint	$3.01	97,480
8			

Using the Fill Handle to Clear Ranges

The fill handle can be used to delete (clear) ranges.

1) Ensure that the range that you want to delete is highlighted.
2) Click and drag the fill handle upwards to delete the cells that you pass through.

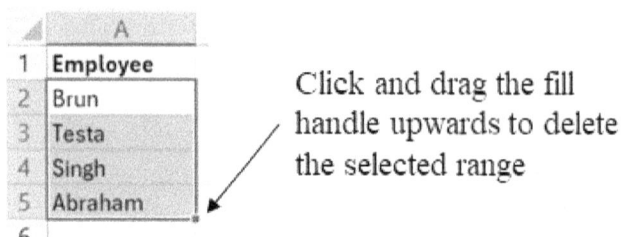

Click and drag the fill handle upwards to delete the selected range

In the above example, cells A2 to A5 have been selected. Clicking and dragging the fill handle, from A5 back up to A2 will clear the contents of this range. Notice that the range becomes shaded as you are dragging the fill handle inside the range.

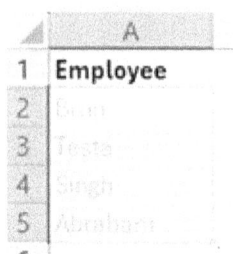

If you drag the fill handle backwards, without a range selected, or if you drag backwards outside the selected range, Excel will try and perform a "reverse fill" if possible, otherwise the data will be copied back up through the range.

Fill Across Worksheets

Fills aren't just up and down – they can work through multiple worksheets too. This is useful when you need the same formulas, contents, or formats in the same location across several sheets.

1) Hold the **CTRL** key and click the sheet tabs you want to include.

2) On the sheet with your formulas or data, select the cells to copy.

3) Select the **Home** tab on the Ribbon, and from the **Editing** group, click on the **Fill** ⬇ ˅ button.

4) Select the **Across Worksheets** option. The "Fill Across Worksheets" dialog box will be displayed.

Fill Across Works...   ?   ✕

Fill

⬤ All
◯ Contents
◯ Formats

OK   Cancel

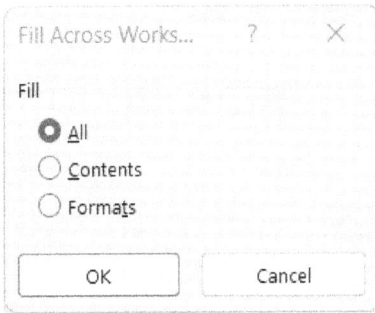

5) Select whether you want to fill the **Contents**, **Formats**, or **All** (both contents and formats) across the selected sheets.

6) Click **OK**.

For example, if Sheet1 has totals in row 10 for columns A to E, highlight those cells, group the other sheets with **CTRL**+click, and use **Fill Across Worksheets** to instantly copy the totals into the same cells on every selected sheet.

EDITING

Controlling the Direction of the Enter Key

By default, Excel moves the cell pointer down one cell whenever you press the **ENTER** key. You can prevent Excel from moving the cell pointer at all when **ENTER** is pressed.

1) Select the **File** tab on the Ribbon and then select the **Options** command.

2) Click on the **Advanced** category.

3) From the **Editing options** section, disable the **After pressing Enter, move selection** option and then click **OK** to return to the worksheet.

Editing options

☑ After pressing Enter, move selection

Direction: [Down ∨]

If you have **After pressing Enter, move selection** enabled, you can use the **Direction** option to specify whether Excel moves the cell pointer **Down**, **Right**, **Up** or **Left** when you press the **ENTER** key.

Data Entry Ranges

When entering a large amount of data, you can first highlight the area where the data will go. As you type each entry, press **ENTER** to move through the selected range.

This method is efficient because when you reach the bottom of a column, pressing **ENTER** automatically takes you to the top of the next column. For example, if you finish in cell B5, the next press of **ENTER** moves you directly to C2, ready for the next entry.

◢	A	B	C	D
1		NSW	QLD	VIC
2	Jan			
3	Feb			
4	Mar			
5	Apr			

Note: If you make a mistake when entering data using this method, press **SHIFT+ENTER** to move back through the selection. Pressing any of the arrow keys when a range is selected will de-select the range.

If you prefer to enter data across rows, instead of down columns, use the **TAB** key to move between the cells. When you reach the end of a selected row, pressing **TAB** takes you to the start of the next row. Use **SHIFT+TAB** to move back through the selection.

Improving Data Entry with the Pick from List Feature

If you start typing the first letter or letters of a value that already exists in the same column, Excel automatically suggests a match. Press **ENTER** to accept the suggestion and complete the entry, or simply keep typing to enter a different value.

	A	B
	Sales Rep	**State**
1	**Sales Rep**	**State**
2	Ryan Nelson	New South Wales
3	Shane Cavers	Queensland
4	Meredith Bassett	Victoria
5	Jillian Howell	South Australia
6	Daniel Price	New South Wales
7	Matthew Connor	

You can also use Excel's **Pick from Drop-down List** feature to help streamline data entry and reduce errors when working with long lists that include repeated values.

Right-click on an empty cell within a column that already contains entries and choose **Pick from Drop-down List** from the shortcut menu. A list of existing values from that column will appear, select the required item using your mouse or the arrow keys and **Enter** to insert it into the cell.

	A	B
1	**Sales Rep**	**State**
2	Ryan Nelson	New South Wales
3	Shane Cavers	Queensland
4	Meredith Bassett	Victoria
5	Jillian Howell	South Australia
6	Daniel Price	
7	Matthew Connor	New South Wales
8		Queensland South Australia
9		Victoria

Note: You can also press **ALT+DOWN ARROW** to activate the list in a cell.

Automatic Pattern Filling with Flash Fill

When you need to reformat or combine text from different columns, Excel's **Flash Fill** can save you from writing complex formulas. Simply type the result you want once, and Excel will do the rest.

For example, if first names are in column A and surnames in column B, type the first full name in column C. As you begin typing the second entry, Excel recognises the pattern and suggests the remaining values. Press **ENTER** to accept the suggestion.

	A	B	C
1	**First Name**	**Surname**	**Full Name**
2	Amos	Hart	Amos Hart
3	Kitai	Raige	Kitai Raige
4	Clarisse	McClellan	Clarisse McClellan
5	Charles	Doren	Charles Doren
6	Jess	Aarons	Jess Aarons
7	Anna	Fitzgerald	Anna Fitzgerald
8	Tommy	DeVito	Tommy DeVito
9	Rachel	Keller	Rachel Keller
10	Evelyn	Salt	Evelyn Salt
11	Leonard	Shelby	Leonard Shelby

Flash Fill can be used for joining or splitting names, reformatting phone numbers, extracting initials, and many other common tasks.

Note: You can also press **CTRL+E** to flash fill the column after typing the first entry.

Entering the Same Data into Multiple Cells

Excel includes a shortcut that lets you enter the same data into multiple cells at once. This is especially useful when working with repeated values. For example, if you are creating a budget and an expense remains the same each month, you can enter it in a single step rather than copying and pasting the value into every cell.

1) Select the cells that you want to enter the data in.

2) Type the data and press **CTRL+ENTER**. The data will be entered into all of the cells that you have highlighted.

Note: This command also works with non-continuous ranges (refer to *"Selecting Non-Continuous Cells"*).

Multiple Lines within a Cell

Excel allows you to split a cell into multiple lines, which can be a useful feature in worksheets where you may have a long column heading, with smaller entries sitting underneath.

Rather than using several rows to accommodate the headings, you can use **ALT+ENTER** to create new lines within a current cell. In the following example you would type the word "Employee" in cell A1, press **ALT+ENTER** and then type the word "Number".

◢	A	B	C
1	Employee Number	First Name	Surname
2	8247	Michelle	Gibbs
3	5150	Gina	Hayden
4	3982	Paul	Sharp

Shortcut for Entering Times

To make entering times faster in Excel, type the time followed by a space and either **a** for AM or **p** for PM.

For example, typing **6 p** (with the space) automatically enters 6:00 PM, while typing **3:10 a** enters 3:10 AM.

When Old Formatting Lingers Behind

When you select a cell or range of cells and press DELETE, only the contents are removed. Any formatting or comments remain in place, which can sometimes lead to unexpected results when you enter new data into that cell.

For example, create a new workbook and enter the date 31/12/25 in cell A1. Click back on cell A1 and press **DELETE** to clear the cell contents. Now type the number 1234 into the same cell and press **ENTER**. Instead of displaying the number, Excel uses the date format (from the previous cell entry), resulting in the display of "18/05/1903".

Excel provides several options for removing data or formatting from selected cells. These options are found under the **Home** tab on the Ribbon, in the **Editing** group, using the **Clear** command.

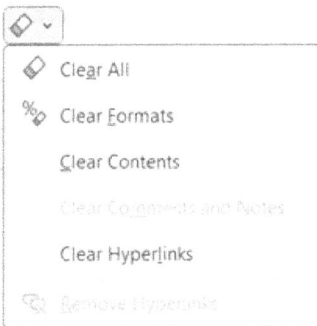

Command	Deletes
Clear All	the cell contents, formatting and comments.
Clear Formats	the formatting of the cell only, the data and comments remain.

Command	Deletes
Clear Contents	the contents of the cell only, the format and cell comments remain (same result as pressing **DELETE** on the keyboard).
Clear Comments and Notes	the comments or notes attached to the cell only, the cell contents and formatting remain.
Clear Hyperlinks	hyperlinks from the selected cells but keeps the displayed text.

Backtracking During a Find or Replace

When you're using the Find or Replace feature in Excel, it's easy to click **Find Next** one time too many and skip past the result you wanted. Fortunately, Excel lets you move backwards through the worksheet.

To do this, simply hold down the **SHIFT** key while clicking **Find Next**.

Excel will then move to the previous match instead of the next one, allowing you to backtrack through your search results.

Inserting a Column from the Keyboard

The following steps describe how to quickly insert a column using keyboard commands.

1) Ensure the cell pointer is positioned in a column to the right of where you want the new column inserted.

2) Press **CTRL+spacebar** to select the entire column.

3) Press **CTRL+SHIFT+equal sign** or **CTRL+plus sign** (numeric keypad) to insert a new column.

Note: You can use a similar technique to insert a row (**SHIFT+spacebar** selects a row), or to delete columns and rows (**CTRL+minus sign** on the numeric keypad to delete).

Inserting Cells

In addition to inserting entire columns and rows, Excel also allows you to insert individual cells. Since a worksheet always contains 16,384 columns and

1,048,576 rows, inserting a cell forces the surrounding cells to shift either down or to the right.

This feature should be used carefully because shifting cells can disrupt formulas, but it is very useful if you realise you missed a value and need to make space for it.

For example in the following diagram, the value for December is missing. As you study the data, you realise that it is actually the data for August that was missed. One alternative solution would be to move the data from cells B8:B11 to B9:B12 (via cut and paste) and then enter the new value in B8 which would then be empty.

	A	B
1	January	62
2	February	45
3	March	22
4	April	79
5	May	87
6	June	38
7	July	18
8	August	39
9	September	51
10	October	17
11	November	28
12	December	

A quicker method (particularly in larger spreadsheets) is to insert a cell at the required location.

1) Click on the location where the new cell is required (in this example B8).

2) Select the **Home** tab, and from the **Cells** group click the **Insert** drop-down arrow and choose **Insert Cells** (you can also right-click on the cell and select **Insert**). The "Insert" dialog box is displayed.

| Insert | ? | X |

Insert

○ Shift cells right
○ Shift cells down
○ Entire row
○ Entire column

| OK | Cancel |

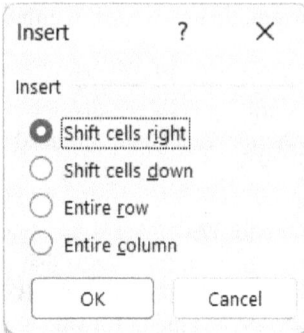

3) Ensure the correct option is selected (in this case to **Shift cells down**) and click **OK**.

Deleting Cells

In the same way that cells can be inserted (refer to "*Inserting Cells*"), they can also be deleted. This can be useful when data entry errors occur.

In the following diagram, the value "12" was entered twice by mistake ("12" should be the value for March and "43" the value for April). As a result of this, there is an additional number at the end of the data entry range (the value "37" belongs to December).

	A	B
1	January	37
2	February	39
3	March	12
4	April	12
5	May	43
6	June	68
7	July	18
8	August	22
9	September	33
10	October	68
11	November	35
12	December	53
13		37

You could delete the data from cell B4 and then move the values from B5:B13 to B4:B12, however the Delete Cells feature achieves both of these actions in one command.

1) Click on the cell you want to delete (in this example B4).

2) Select the **Home** tab, and from the **Cells** group click the **Delete** drop-down arrow and choose **Delete Cells** (you can also right-click on the cell and select **Insert**). The "Delete" dialog box is displayed.

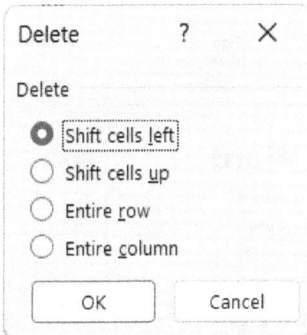

3) Ensure the correct option is selected (in this case to **Shift cells up**) and click **OK**.

Searching Across Worksheets

When performing a "find" operation, Excel allows you to specify whether you want the search to be restricted to the one worksheet, or conducted over the entire workbook.

1) Select the **Home** tab, then from the **Editing** group, click **Find & Select** and then click **Find** (or use the keyboard shortcut **CTRL+F**). The "Find and Replace" dialog box is displayed.

2) If necessary, click the **Options >>** button to expand the dialog box.

3) Click on the drop-down arrow next to the **Within** field, and select either **Sheet** or **Workbook**.

Find and Replace   □   ✕

Fin_d_   Re_p_lace

Fi_n_d what: [   ] ⌄   [No Format Set]   [For_m_at... ▾]

Wit_h_in: [Sheet   ⌄]   ☐ Match _c_ase
          [Sheet   ]   ☐ Match entire cell co_n_tents
_S_earch: [Workbook   ]
_L_ook in: [Formulas   ⌄]   Op_t_ions <<

                    Fi_n_d All   _F_ind Next   Close

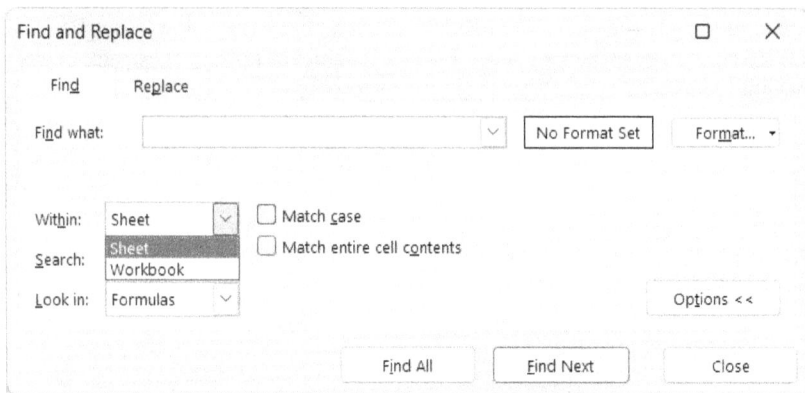

Finding All Occurrences of a Word

Excel's Find feature makes it easy to quickly locate and move to every occurrence of a particular text string within a worksheet.

1) Select the **Home** tab, then from the **Editing** group, click **Find & Select** and then click **Find** (or use the keyboard shortcut CTRL+F). The "Find and Replace" dialog box is displayed.

2) Enter the text you are searching for in the **Find what** field.

3) Click the **Find All** button.

The dialog box expands to show a list of all the found matches. Clicking on the items in the list selects the relevant cell in the worksheet.

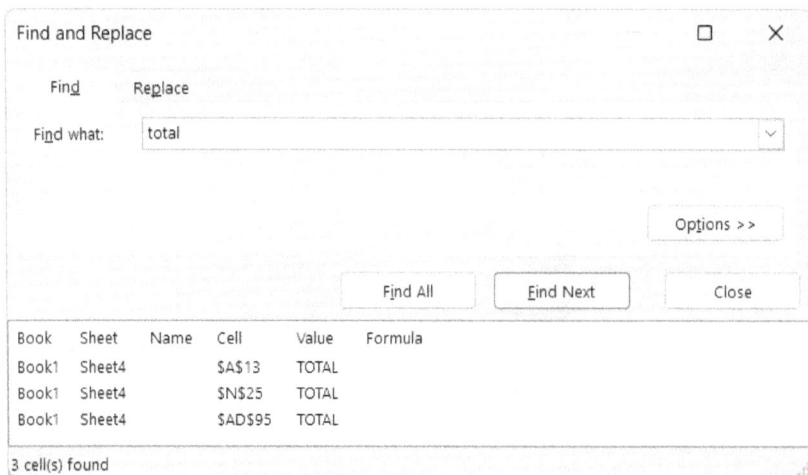

Find and Replace   □   ✕

Fin_d_   Re_p_lace

Fi_n_d what: [total   ] ⌄

                                        Op_t_ions >>

                    Fi_n_d All   _F_ind Next   Close

Book	Sheet	Name	Cell	Value	Formula
Book1	Sheet4		$A$13	TOTAL	
Book1	Sheet4		$N$25	TOTAL	
Book1	Sheet4		$AD$95	TOTAL	

3 cell(s) found

Modifying a Range Reference in a Formula

When you edit a formula in Excel, each cell reference in the Formula Bar is shown in a different colour. The corresponding cells on the worksheet are outlined with matching coloured borders, which makes it easier to see and adjust the references in the formula.

1) Select a cell containing a formula and press **F2** (or double-click the cell) to enter edit mode. Excel highlights each range in the formula with a coloured border around the referenced cells.

2) Locate the coloured border for the range you want to modify.

3) Using the mouse, drag the border handles (small squares on the corners) to adjust the selection to the new range.

4) Press **ENTER** to confirm your changes. Excel automatically updates the formula with the new cell reference based on the adjusted range.

Cloning a Formula Across a Range of Cells

You can create a formula across a range of cells by using the keyboard command **CTRL+ENTER**.

In the following example, we want to multiply the values in column A by the values in column B (ie: in C1 we want the answer to A1*B1, in C2 we want the answer to A2*B2, etc.).

	A	B	C
1	19	7	
2	21	4	
3	26	9	
4	14	5	
5	18	6	

1) Highlight all the cells where answers are required (cells C1 to C5 in this example).

2) Enter the formula for the first cell (in this example =A1*B1) and press **CTRL+ENTER**.

Separate formulas are created for each cell that you highlighted.

C4		⌄ ⋮ X ✓	*fx* ⌄	=A4*B4
◢	A	B	C	D
1	19	7	133	
2	21	4	84	
3	26	9	234	
4	14	5	70	
5	18	6	108	

Quickly Duplicate Data with Keyboard Shortcuts

To quickly duplicate the entry from the cell directly above the current cell, press **CTRL+D**. For example, in the following diagram, pressing **CTRL+D** in the active cell (C5) would duplicate the value from cell C4 (48).

◢	A	B	C
1		2024 Sales by Re	
2			
3		Qtr 1	Qtr 2
4	North	40	48
5	South	41	
6	East	47	
7	West	34	
8	Total	162	

You can also duplicate the entry from the cell directly to the left of the current cell, using the keyboard command **CTRL+R**. For example, in the above diagram, pressing **CTRL+R** in the active cell (C5) would duplicate the value from cell B5 (41).

In both cases, if the cell you are duplicating contains a formula, Excel duplicates the formula in the same way as it would if you had copied and pasted the cell (ie: follows the absolute v relative referencing rules).

You can duplicate a value (or a formula) into multiple cells by selecting the cell containing the data you want to duplicate and the blank cells where you want the data to go. In the following example, pressing **CTRL+D** would fill the formula from the current cell into the selected cells below.

| C2 | ⌄ : ✕ ✓ *fx* ⌄ | =B2+($C$9*B2) |

	A	B	C	D
1		January	February	
2	SummitPath	1000	1100	
3	BrightWave	800		
4	HorizonFlex	650		
5	SkillForge	1200		
6	PureFlow	1450		
7	BluePeak	790		
8				
9	Forecast Increase		10%	

Pressing **CTRL+R** in the following example would duplicate the formula into the cells selected on the right.

| B11 | ⌄ : ✕ ✓ *fx* ⌄ | =AVERAGE(B2:B7) |

	A	B	C	D	E	F	G
1		January	February	March	April	May	June
2	SummitPath	1000	1,100	1,210	1,331	1,464	1,611
3	BrightWave	800	880	968	1,065	1,171	1,288
4	HorizonFlex	650	715	787	865	952	1,047
5	SkillForge	1200	1,320	1,452	1,597	1,757	1,933
6	PureFlow	1450	1,595	1,755	1,930	2,123	2,335
7	BluePeak	790	869	956	1,051	1,157	1,272
8							
9	Forecast Increase		10%				
10							
11	AVERAGE	982					

Copying from the Cell Directly Above

The following two shortcuts allow you to copy from the cell directly above the active cell.

CTRL+'   Copies the entry from the cell above. If the entry is a formula, an identical copy of the formula is copied (ie: there is no adjusting of cell references).

CTRL+SHIFT+'   Copies the entry from the cell above. If the entry is a formula, the result of the formula (the value) is copied.

Copying a Formula Down a Column

Worksheets often contain formulas that need to be copied down a column. While there are several ways to do this, the quickest is to use the Fill Handle. You can drag the Fill Handle to extend the formula, but this becomes impractical if you are working with hundreds or even thousands of rows.

The fastest way to copy a formula down a column is to **double-click the Fill Handle**. Excel automatically fills the formula downward as long as it detects data in the adjacent column to the left. The process stops when Excel encounters a blank cell in that column.

D2			f_x	=B2*C2

	A	B	C	D
1	Employee	Rate	Hours	Gross Pay
2	Balasuryia	$ 24.95	32	$798.40
3	Powter	$ 31.19	27.5	
4	Sortwell	$ 28.20	40	
5	Woodhouse	$ 28.44	28	
6				
7	TOTALS			

Double-click the Fill Handle to copy the formula down the column

In the example above, the formula in cell D2 multiplies the rate (B2) by the hours (C2). Double-clicking the fill handle in cell D2 would copy the formula down as far as D5 (the blank cell C6 causes it to stop).

Copying Only Visible Cells

When you copy cells that contain hidden rows or columns, Excel also copies the hidden data along with the visible cells. This often creates problems when working with subtotalled or filtered lists.

In the example below, a list of data has been sub-totalled and level 2 totals are displayed. Selecting and copying the four region total headings and values would include the data in the range B169 to C508.

1 2 3	◢	A	B	C
	1	**Person**	**Region**	**Sales**
+	169		East Total	$60,373
+	338		North Total	$62,156
+	423		South Total	$29,666
+	508		West Total	$27,912
−	509		Grand Total	$180,107

The following steps describe how to select only the visible (ie: non hidden) cells.

1) Highlight the area to copy (in this example B169 to C508).

2) Press **F5** (Go To).

3) Click on the **Special** button and select the **Visible cells only** option.

4) Click **OK**. Only the contents of the visible (non-hidden) cells are selected.

The data can then be copied and pasted successfully.

Pasting Values Instead of Formulas

Some formulas in Excel are designed to transform or replace the original data they reference, for example, CONCATENATE, TEXTJOIN, UPPER, LOWER, PROPER and RAND (refer to "*Joining Cells Together*", "*Converting the Case of Text*" and "*Creating Random Numbers*" for further information on these functions).

The limitation of these formulas is that they depend on the original data remaining in place. If a referenced cell is deleted, the formula will return an error. One temporary solution is to hide the columns that contain the source data. A more permanent solution is to copy the results of the formulas and then paste them back into the worksheet as values.

In the following example, the formulas in column D join together the names in columns A, B and C, converting them to uppercase and removing any excess spaces.

| | D2 | | ⌄ | ⋮ | ✕ | ✓ | *fx* | ⌄ | =UPPER(TEXTJOIN(" ", TRUE, TRIM(A2), TRIM(B2), TRIM(C2))) |

	A	B	C	D	E	F
1	First Name	Middle Initial	Surname	Full Name		
2	Meredith		Bassett	MEREDITH BASSETT		
3	Kin		Lin	KIN LIN		
4	Valnea	J.	Peresson	VALNEA J. PERESSON		
5	David		Connor	DAVID CONNOR		
6	Jim	A.	Pope	JIM A. POPE		
7	Shivali		Raina	SHIVALI RAINA		
8	Glen		Arnold	GLEN ARNOLD		

Now that the full names have been created, there is no need for the information in columns A through C. However, because the full names are the result of a formula that uses data from these columns, the data must remain present, otherwise formula errors will result. To work around this problem the formulas from column D are copied and then pasted back as values.

1) Highlight the cells containing the formulas (cells D2:D8 in the above example).

2) Copy the cell contents to the clipboard.

3) Keeping the range selected, select the **Home** tab on the Ribbon and from the **Clipboard** group, click the drop-down arrow under **Paste** (the clipboard icon) and choose the **Values** option, as shown below.

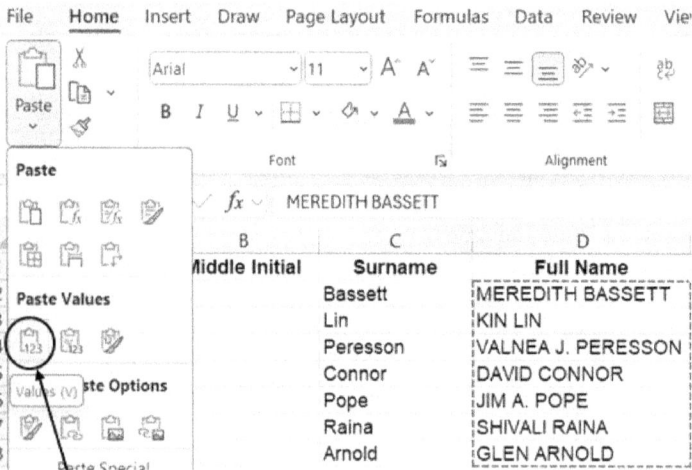

Paste Values option

4) The original data can then be deleted (in this example columns A through C can be removed).

Note: This feature can be a useful method of preventing random numbers from changing. By default, random numbers that are created using the RAND, RANDARRAY and RANDBETWEEN functions change each time the spreadsheet is recalculated.

Convert Formulas to Values with a Right-Click

A quick method of converting formula results to values is available using the right mouse button.

1) Select the range of cells containing the formulas to be converted into values.

2) Right-click and drag the border of the range one cell in any direction (without letting go of the mouse) and then return the range back to its original location.

3) Release the mouse button. Excel displays a shortcut menu (as shown below). The **Copy Here as Values Only** option is the equivalent of pasting as values.

D2		✓ ⨉ ✓ fx ✓	=UPPER(TEXTJOIN(" ", TRUE, TRIM(A2), TRIM(B2), TRIM(C2)))				
	A	B	C	D	E	F	G
1	First Name	Middle Initial	Surname	Full Name			
2	Meredith		Bassett	MEREDITH BASSETT			
3	Kin		Lin	KIN LIN			
4	Valnea	J.	Peresson D2:D8	VALNEA J. PERESSON	Move Here		
5	David		Connor	DAVID CONNOR			
6	Jim	A.	Pope	JIM A. POPE	Copy Here		
7	Shivali		Raina	SHIVALI RAINA			
8	Glen		Arnold	GLEN ARNOLD	Copy Here as Values Only		
9					Copy Here as Formats Only		
10					Link Here		
11							
12					Create Hyperlink Here		
13							
14							
15							
16							
17							
18							
19							
20					Cancel		

Paste Options

The **Paste** button on the **Home** tab of the Ribbon contains a drop down arrow that allows you to select various methods of pasting data (e.g., Values, Formulas, Formatting).

After you paste data, a **Paste Options button** (a small clipboard icon) appears near the data that you have pasted. This button offers different choices depending on the type of data being pasted.

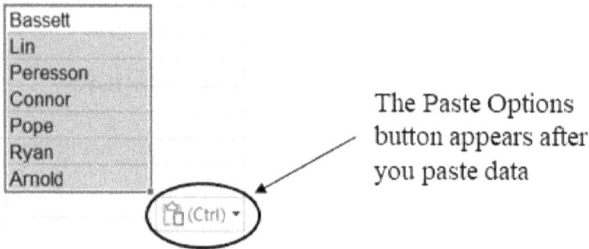

| Bassett |
| Lin |
| Peresson |
| Connor |
| Pope |
| Ryan |
| Arnold |

The Paste Options button appears after you paste data

The Paste Options button disappears once you perform your next action in Excel. If you prefer, you can permanently disable this feature by following these steps:

1) Select the **File** tab on the Ribbon and then select the **Options** command.

2) Click on the **Advanced** category.

3) From the **Cut, Copy, and Paste** section, disable the **Show Paste Options button when content is pasted** option.

4) Click **OK** to apply the change.

Note: Disabling the **Paste Options** button also disables the Auto Fill Options button, which appears after you use the fill handle to copy or extend data.

Dragging & Dropping Cells

An easy way to move a single cell or a range of cells is with the Drag & Drop technique. This method is especially useful if you've entered data in the wrong place and need to reposition it instantly.

1) Select the cell or range you want to move.

2) Hover the mouse pointer over the border of the selected cell(s). The pointer will change to a four-sided arrow.

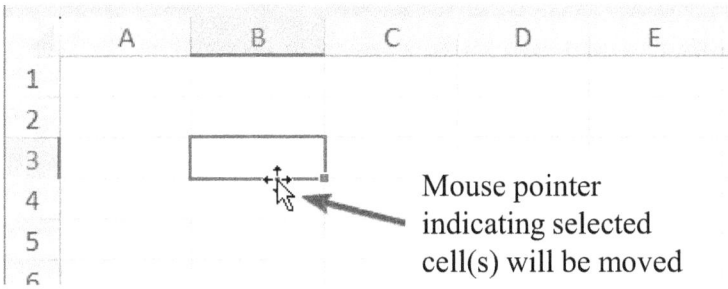

Mouse pointer
indicating selected
cell(s) will be moved

3) Click and hold the left mouse button, then drag the selection to its new location. An outline of the data will move with your cursor, helping you position it accurately.

4) Release the mouse button to drop the data into the new location.

Note: To copy cells using drag & drop, perform the above steps whilst holding down the **CTRL** key. Ensure that you have the **CTRL** key held down for the duration of the copying process (ie: release the mouse button first and then release the **CTRL** key). A small plus symbol (+) will appear next to the four-sided arrow as you drag & drop to inform you that you are copying the selected cell(s).

Dragging & Dropping Between Sheets

You can use the Drag & Drop technique with the **ALT** key to quickly move information between different sheets of your workbook.

1) Select the range to be moved to another sheet.

2) Holding down the **ALT** key on the keyboard, drag the data over the top of the sheet tab representing the sheet where you want to move the data to. This sheet will be activated.

3) Release the **ALT** key.

4) Continue dragging to ensure the information is placed in the correct location on the new sheet.

Note: To copy information between sheets, hold down **CTRL** and **ALT** whilst dragging information between sheets.

Dragging & Dropping with the Right Mouse Button

If you drag & drop data using the right mouse button, Excel displays a shortcut menu when you release the mouse button. This menu allows you to select from a range of actions that can be applied to the cell(s) that have been dragged and dropped.

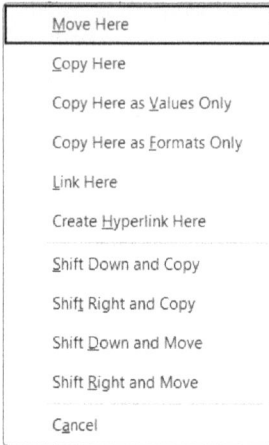

Move Here
Copy Here
Copy Here as Values Only
Copy Here as Formats Only
Link Here
Create Hyperlink Here
Shift Down and Copy
Shift Right and Copy
Shift Down and Move
Shift Right and Move
Cancel

Cutting, Dragging & Dropping

Holding down the **SHIFT** key whilst dragging and dropping enables you to cut data from the original cell(s) and insert it in the destination cell(s). For example, in the following diagram the contents of cell B3 are cut from the cell and inserted at B7. Employee "Nelson" moves to the bottom of the list, the other employees each move up one cell.

	A	B
1		
2	Emp#	Name
3	101	Nelson
4	102	Jones
5	103	Smith
6	104	Jackson

The original data

	A	B
1		
2	Emp#	Name
3	101	Nelson
4	102	Jones
5	103	Smith
6	104	Jackson
7		
8		B7

Data being dragged
and dropped, using
the **SHIFT** key

	A	B
1		
2	Emp#	Name
3	101	Jones
4	102	Smith
5	103	Jackson
6	104	Nelson

The re-arranged data

Note: You can also copy cells and insert them using drag & drop, by holding down **CTRL+SHIFT** whilst dragging and dropping.

Easily Re-Order Worksheet Columns

Have you ever needed to change the order of columns in your worksheet? The usual approach is to insert blank columns and then cut and paste data, but there's a much faster technique – you can simply drag and drop entire columns into the order you want.

1) Select the column(s) you want to move.

2) Hover over the border of your selection (the selected cells, not the column header) until the cursor changes to a four-headed arrow, as shown in the following diagram.

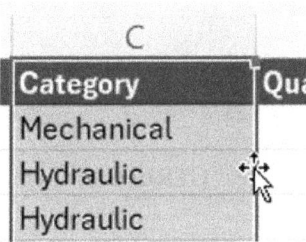

C	
Category	Qua
Mechanical	
Hydraulic	
Hydraulic	

3) Hold down **SHIFT** then click and drag the column to its new position. A faint vertical "I" bar will appear showing where the column will be placed.

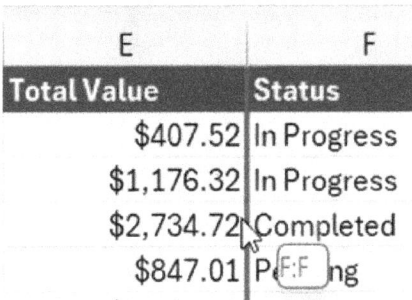

E	F
Total Value	Status
$407.52	In Progress
$1,176.32	In Progress
$2,734.72	Completed
$847.01	P F:F ng

4) Release the mouse button before releasing the **SHIFT** key.

Collecting and Pasting

The Office Clipboard allows you to collect and store up to 24 copied or cut items from any program that supports the Copy or Cut command. You can then paste any or all of those items into an Office application such as Excel, Word, PowerPoint, Access, or Outlook.

For example, you can copy a chart in Excel, a list from PowerPoint, and some text from a website, then paste them all into your Excel worksheet.

1) Select the **Home** tab on the Ribbon and from the **Clipboard** group click the **Clipboard launcher** button (small diagonal arrow in the bottom-right corner). The Clipboard pane will be displayed.

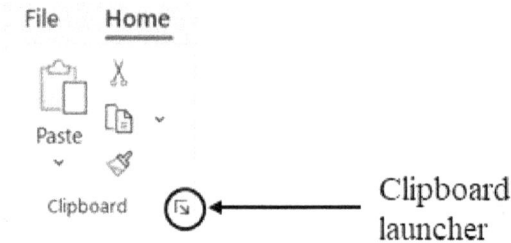

2) Select the first item you want to copy and press **CTRL+C** (or right-click and select **Copy**).

3) Repeat for each additional item (up to 24 items). Each copied item appears in the Clipboard pane.

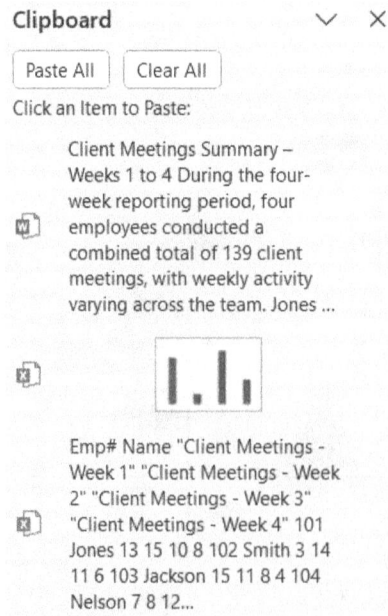

4) Click the **Paste All** button at the top of the Clipboard pane to paste all collected items in sequence, or click a single item from the list to paste it at the current cursor position.

Repeating Commands with One Key

If you need to perform the same action several times in succession, such as deleting a column, removing a row or applying formatting, Excel's repeat feature can save you time.

In the following example, the blank rows between each set of data need to be deleted.

8	1st Quarter	123,000	85,000	38,000
9				
10	2nd Quarter	132,000	63,000	69,000
11				
12	3rd Quarter	156,000	58,000	98,000
13				
14	4th Quarter	121,000	45,000	76,000

1) Click on row heading **9** to select the entire row.

2) Right-click over the row heading and select **Delete**.

3) Click on the row heading of the next blank row you want to remove (which will now be row **10**, as the rows move up after deletion).

4) Press **F4** on the keyboard to repeat the last command.

5) Click on the row heading of the next blank row you want to remove (which will now be row **11**).

6) Press **F4** on the keyboard to repeat the last command.

Note: The repeat (**F4**) command will only repeat the last action made. If you want to apply multiple formatting changes (eg: bold and italics) you have to open the appropriate dialog box and make the changes. This ensures that all the changes are considered as one action by Excel and they will be repeated. If you make the same changes on the toolbar, only the last change made is stored as the action to repeat.

Switching Rows to Columns or Columns to Rows

Excel's **Transpose** feature allows you to switch the layout of your spreadsheet, ie: data from the top row of the spreadsheet appears in the left column of the new area and data from the left column appears in the top row.

The following steps describe how to use the transpose feature.

1) Select the range of cells that you want to re-arrange and copy them to the clipboard.

2) Select a blank cell in the top left hand corner of the area where you want to paste the data.

3) Select the **Home** tab, and from the **Clipboard** group, click the **Paste** drop-down arrow and select the **Transpose** option.

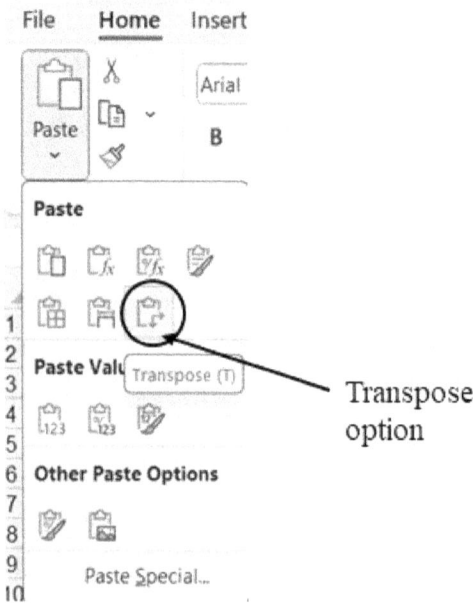

The following diagram shows the results of the transpose feature. The top part of the diagram shows the original layout of the data, the second part of the diagram shows the transposed data.

	A	B	C	D	E	F	G
1		Books	Videos	Magazines			
2	January	242	239	288			
3	February	205	382	97			
4	March	326	178	355			
5	April	220	344	306			
6	May	210	184	286			
7	June	312	156	286			
8							
9		January	February	March	April	May	June
10	Books	242	205	326	220	210	312
11	Videos	239	382	178	344	184	156
12	Magazines	288	97	355	306	286	286

WORKING WITH WORKBOOKS

Creating a New Worksheet

A quick way to add a new worksheet to the current workbook is to use the keyboard command **SHIFT+F11**. The new sheet is added before the currently selected sheet.

Grouping Worksheets Together

When you want to use the same feature on multiple worksheets, you can "group" them together.

If the sheets you want to work with are located together, click on the first sheet tab that you require in the group, hold down **SHIFT** on the keyboard and click on the last sheet tab you require – Excel groups together all the sheets between (and including) the first sheet and the last sheet you selected.

If the sheets that you want to group are not located together you can use the **CTRL** key to select individual sheets for the group.

Excel displays a message in the title bar to indicate the sheets are grouped.

Once the sheets are grouped you can perform many different actions that will affect all of the selected sheets, for example;
- Entering data into cells
- Deleting data from cells
- Formatting cells
- Changing column widths and row heights
- Inserting or deleting columns
- Printing the selected sheets
- Inserting or deleting sheets.

To ungroup sheets, click on a sheet tab that is not part of the group. If all of the sheets in the workbook are grouped, clicking on any sheet tab will ungroup the sheets. You can also right-click over one of the grouped sheet tabs and select the **Ungroup Sheets** command from the shortcut menu.

Insert...

Delete

Rename

Move or Copy...

View Code

Protect Sheet...

Tab Color   >

Hide

Unhide...

Select All Sheets

Ungroup Sheets

Sheet3   S...

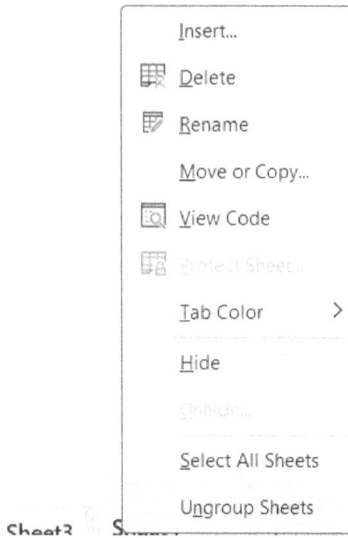

Selecting a Group Of Sheets

If you need to select multiple sheets from a workbook that includes most, but not all of the sheets, you can use the following technique

1) Select all sheets by right-clicking on any sheet tab and choosing **Select All Sheets** from the shortcut menu.

2) While holding down the **CTRL** key, click on the sheet tabs you don't want included in the group to deselect them.

Note: To select a few individual sheets without selecting them all first, hold down **CTRL** while clicking each sheet tab you want to include in your selection. You can also select a continuous group of sheets by clicking the first sheet, holding **SHIFT**, and then clicking the last sheet in the range.

Adjusting the Number of Sheets in a New Workbook

By default, new workbooks in Excel contain one worksheet. You can change this default setting to automatically include more sheets whenever you create a new workbook.

1) Select the **File** tab on the Ribbon and then select the **Options** command.

2) Click on the **General** category.

3) From the section **When creating new workbooks** enter the number of sheets you want (between 1 and 255) in the **Include this many sheets** field and click **OK** to apply your changes.

Note: You can also add or remove sheets in a workbook at any time by clicking the "+" icon next to the sheet tabs, or by right-clicking an existing sheet tab and selecting **Insert** or **Delete**.

Adjusting the Number of Sheet Tabs Displayed

You can change how much space is allocated to display the sheet tabs at the bottom of the workbook. Expanding this area allows more tabs to be visible at once, but it also reduces the width of the horizontal scroll bar.

To adjust the size of the sheet tab area, position the mouse pointer in the gap between the sheet tabs and the scroll bar (called the tab split box), and then click and drag.

Dubbo   Newcastle   Wagga ⋯   +

Position the mouse pointer here and then click and drag to adjust the display of sheet tabs

To restore the default setting for this feature, double-click on the tab split box.

Coloured Sheet Tabs

You can colour code the sheet tabs for easier identification or grouping of related sheets.

1) Select the sheet tab(s) that you want to colour. Refer to "*Grouping Worksheets Together*" for further information on selecting multiple sheets.

2) Right-click on one of the selected sheet tabs and select **Tab Color** from the shortcut menu.

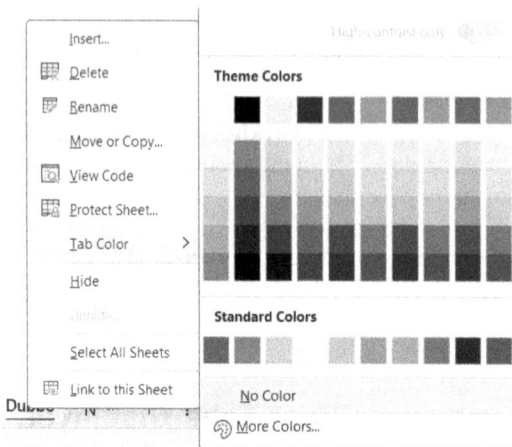

3) Select the required colour and click **OK**.

You can remove colour from a sheet tab by following the above procedure and selecting the **No Color** option.

Coloured sheet tabs that are selected appear with the colour underlining the sheet name.

Re-Arranging Worksheets

You can change the order of worksheets within a workbook or even move them to another file.

The quickest way is to click and drag a worksheet tab to the desired location. As you drag, a small black triangle appears above the tabs to show where the sheet will be placed.

Alternatively, you can right-click a worksheet tab and choose **Move or Copy** to reposition the sheet within the workbook or transfer it to a different workbook. This command allows you to move the sheet to another workbook via the **To book** command.

Move or Copy   ?   ✕

Move selected sheets

To book:

| Book1 | ⌄ |

Before sheet:

| Sheet1 |
| Sheet3 |
| Sheet2 |
| Sheet4 |
| (move to end) |

☐ Create a copy

| OK | Cancel |

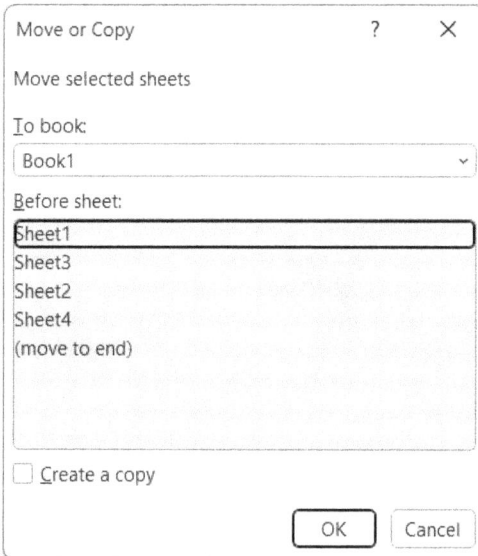

Duplicating Worksheets

Instead of copying and pasting all the data from one sheet to another, Excel lets you duplicate entire worksheets with ease. This is particularly useful when you need multiple sheets based on the same model, such as a template for monthly financial reports.

The quickest method of copying a worksheet is to click and drag the sheet tab to a new position in the workbook, whilst holding down the **CTRL** key on the keyboard.

You can also right-click over the worksheet tab and select the **Move or Copy** command, enabling the **Create a copy** option. This command also allows you to move or copy the sheet to another workbook via the **To book** command.

```
Move or Copy                    ?    ✕

Move selected sheets

To book:
┌──────────────────────────────────────┐
│ Book1                              ⌄  │
└──────────────────────────────────────┘
Before sheet:
┌──────────────────────────────────────┐
│ Sheet1                                │
│ Sheet3                                │
│ Sheet2                                │
│ Sheet4                                │
│ (move to end)                         │
│                                       │
│                                       │
└──────────────────────────────────────┘
☑ Create a copy

              ┌──────────┐  ┌──────────┐
              │    OK    │  │  Cancel  │
              └──────────┘  └──────────┘
```

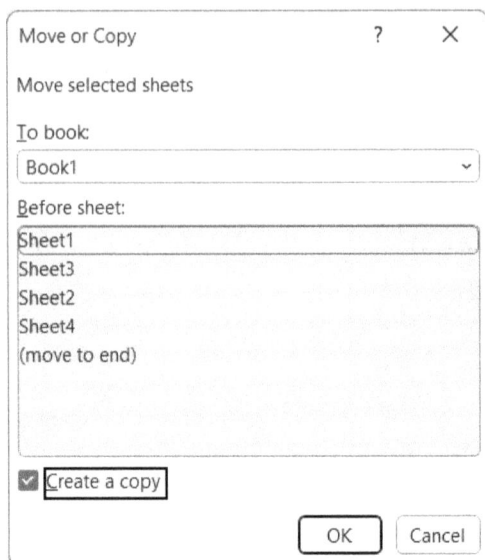

Note: After copying a worksheet, the new worksheet will have the original worksheet tab name, with the addition of a **(2)** to indicate that it is a duplicate. A worksheet tab can be renamed by double-clicking on it.

Moving and Copying Worksheets Between Workbooks

In addition to being able to move and copy worksheets within a workbook via drag & drop (refer to "*Re-Arranging Worksheets*"), you can also drag worksheets to other open workbooks.

The following steps describe how to move a worksheet from one file to another.

1) Ensure both files (source and destination) are open.

2) Arrange the files so that both can be seen on the screen at the same time (use the **Arrange All** command from the **View** tab.).

3) Drag and drop the sheet tab from the source file to the destination file.

Note: To copy a worksheet from one workbook to another, hold down the **CTRL** key whilst dragging the sheet tab.

The source file must contain more than one worksheet if you are moving the sheet tab, ie: you cannot remove the only sheet from a workbook.

These techniques can be used with multiple worksheets (refer to "*Grouping Worksheets Together*").

Automatically Opening Workbooks When Excel Starts

You can configure Excel to automatically open one or more specific workbooks each time you launch the program by specifying a startup folder.

1) Create a folder to store any workbooks you want Excel to open automatically
   (if you don't already have one).

2) Move or copy the desired workbook files into this folder.

3) Select the **File** tab on the Ribbon and then select the **Options** command.

4) Click on the **Advanced** category.

5) Scroll down to the **General** group and in the field **At startup, open all files in:**, enter the full path to the folder you created in step 1.

General

☐ Ignore other applications that use Dynamic Data Exchange (DDE)

☑ Ask to update automatic links

☐ Show add-in user interface errors

☑ Scale content for A4 or 8.5 x 11" paper sizes

☐ Always open encrypted files in this app

At startup, open all files in: | C:\Sales Data\Daily Sales Reports |

6) Click **OK** to save your changes.

Note: Every time you start Excel, all files in that folder will open automatically. To stop this, simply remove the files from the folder or delete the reference to the **At startup, open all files in: folder**.

Cycling Through Open Files

If you have several spreadsheet files open at the same time, use **CTRL+F6** to cycle forward through the open files and **CTRL+SHIFT+F6** to cycle through the open files in the opposite direction.

You can also use the **CTRL+TAB** and **CTRL+SHIFT+TAB** commands to perform the same functions.

Displaying Range Names when Zooming In on a Sheet

You can adjust the zoom level of your worksheet to make the content appear larger or smaller:

Use the Zoom slider located in the bottom-right corner of the Excel window. Drag the slider left to zoom out or right to zoom in.

The Zoom slider area

Alternatively, go to the **View** tab on the Ribbon and select **Zoom**, then choose your preferred zoom level or enter a custom percentage.

You can also hold down **CTRL** and scroll your mouse wheel up or down to adjust the zoom quickly.

When the zoom percentage is **39** (or less), Excel displays any named ranges (refer to "*Using the Name Box*" for further information on creating a named range) in the spreadsheet in blue lettering in the appropriate places.

Note: You must be in Normal view, not Page Break Preview to see the range names displayed.

Range names only appear on the screen – they do not print with your data.

Hiding Zero Values

By default, Excel displays zeros in cells, whether you type them directly or they appear as the result of a formula. If a cell is left empty, it remains blank. There may be situations, however, where you prefer not to show zero values. The steps below explain how to hide them.

1) Select the **File** tab on the Ribbon and then select the **Options** command.

2) Click on the **Advanced** category.

3) Scroll down to the **Display options for this worksheet** section and disable the **Show a zero in cells that have zero value** option.

4) Click **OK** to apply the change.

Note: The setting of the **Zero Values** option affects both the on screen display and the printing of zero values. If zero values are not displayed on screen, they will not be printed either.

Displaying Two Worksheets at Once

Sometimes it is helpful to view two worksheets from the same workbook at the same time. For example, you may want to compare figures from one month with those from another. Excel does not include a built-in command for this, but you can use a simple workaround to make it possible.

1) Ensure the file containing the sheets you want to arrange is open.

2) Select the **View** tab on the Ribbon and from the **Window** group select **New Window**. This opens a second window of the same workbook.

3) From the **Window** group, select the **Arrange All** command. The "Arrange Windows" dialog box will be displayed.

4) Select a window arrangement that suits the spreadsheet you are working on
(eg: vertical).

5) Ensure the **Windows of active workbook** option is enabled. This ensures that the arrangement of windows only includes those of the current file (ignoring other currently open files).

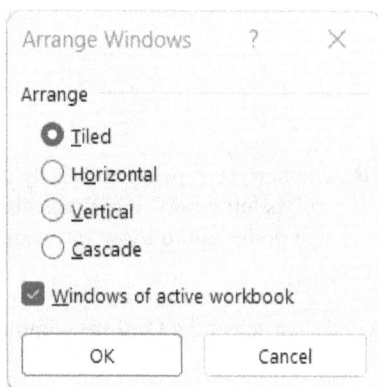

6) Click **OK**.

7) You can display different worksheets in each of the windows simply by activating the window and clicking on the worksheet tab that you want to display.

8) To return to a single window view of the spreadsheet, close the additional windows, ensuring that one window is displayed (if you close all of the windows you will be in effect closing the file).

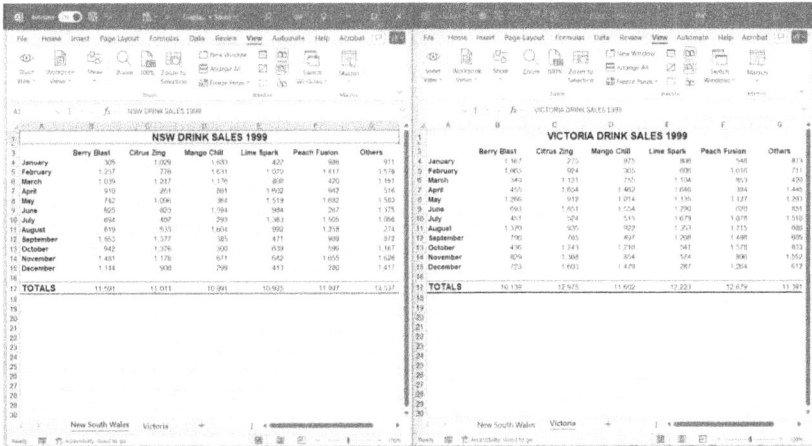

Freezing Worksheet Titles on the Screen

When working with large worksheets, the row and column headings often disappear from view as you scroll. To keep them visible, you can "freeze" the headings so they remain in place while you move through the rest of the worksheet.

1) Position the cell pointer in a position where the headings that you want to freeze are located directly above and directly to the left of the cell.

	A	B	C	D	E
1		Jan-24	Feb-24	Mar-24	Apr-24
2	Product 1	15,214	671	16,768	678
3	Product 2	690	252	14,788	1,205
4	Product 3	232	11,344	18,823	19,255
5	Product 4	9,739	7,394	6,546	13,249
6	Product 5	12,661	17,162	12,529	11,573
7	Product 6	3,521	18,775	3,273	3,765
8	Product 7	13,347	3,650	2,624	17,902

In the above diagram the cell pointer is positioned in cell B2 so that the headings to be frozen appear in the rows above and the columns to the left of the cell pointer.

2) Go to the **View** tab on the Ribbon and in the **Window** group, click the **Freeze Panes** button. You can select to:

Freeze Panes – Freezes both rows and columns above and to the left of the selected cell.

Freeze Top Row – Keeps only the top row visible while scrolling.

Freeze First Column – Keeps only the first column visible while scrolling.

In this example, **Freeze Panes** was selected. Thin black lines will appear around the frozen titles.

3) As you move around the spreadsheet, the titles will remain in position.

	A	T	U	V	W
1		**Jul-25**	**Aug-25**	**Sep-25**	**Oct-25**
56	Product 55	16,605	496	12,525	16,837
57	Product 56	14,592	17,118	10,576	18,147
58	Product 57	18,069	7,224	4,467	17,013
59	Product 58	8,710	4,567	16,093	8,234
60	Product 59	6,226	11,473	10,280	4,565
61	Product 60	6,232	15,392	2,673	15,348
62	Product 61	17,393	14,417	5,941	969
63	Product 62	10,073	10,908	216	1,376
64	Product 63	3,972	8,796	5,184	13,943

Note: To remove the titles go to the **View** tab on the Ribbon and in the **Window** group, select the **Freeze Panes** button and then select the **Unfreeze Panes** command.

Titles frozen with this command do not get repeated on each page of a printout (refer to "*Setting Print Ranges and Titles Using Named Ranges*" for further information on setting print titles).

Splitting the Window

You can split the Excel window into different sections (called panes) to compare areas of the spreadsheet that you would not normally see together.

1) Position the cell pointer in the worksheet:

To split both rows and columns, click the cell below and to the right of where you want the split to occur.

To split only rows, select the cell just below the row where you want the split.

To split only columns, select the cell just to the right of the column where you want the split.

2) Go to the **View** tab on the Ribbon and in the **Window** group, click **Split**. Excel inserts splitter lines on the worksheet:

A horizontal grey line appears above the selected row to separate panes vertically.

A vertical grey line appears to the left of the selected column to separate panes horizontally.

If you selected a cell that allows both, you will see both lines, dividing the screen into four sections.

3) Each pane can be scrolled independently, letting you view different parts of the worksheet side by side.

⟋	A	B	C	D
1		Jan-24	Feb-24	Feb-25
2	Product 1	15,214	671	3,375
3	Product 2	690	252	8,443
4	Product 3	232	11,344	728
5	Product 4	9,739	7,394	12,724
6	Product 5	12,661	17,162	2,997
7	Product 6	3,521	18,775	1,872
8	Product 7	13,347	3,650	11,017

Splitter line

This screen is split so that Feb-24 and Feb-25 can be compared side-by-side

Note: To remove the split windows, double-click on the split bar. If you have the window split in both directions at the same time, double-click on the intersection of the split bars to remove both of them.

Viewing Results in Cells Without Scrolling

Excel allows you to keep an eye on the current values in key cells without having to scroll to the cells themselves. You can even watch values on other sheets or in other workbooks (provided the workbook is currently open).

For example, entering data in row 162 may affect the result of a formula in cell H1. Rather than scrolling back to H1 to see the result of the formula update, you can "watch" the value of the formula change from within the window, no matter where you are on the worksheet.

To add a cell to the watch window, select the cell and then select the **Formulas** tab, and from the **Formula Auditing** group, click **Watch Window**. The "Watch Window" toolbar will be displayed.

Click the **Add Watch** button and then the **Add** button to add the currently selected cell(s) to the Watch Window.

Watch Window					⌄ ✕
?⌂ Add Watch...	✕ Delete Watch				
Book	Sheet	Name	Cell	Value	Formula
Watch ...	Sales D...		H1	$82,347,525	=SUM(E2:E225)
Watch ...	Sales D...		H3	27,449,175	=SUM(D2:D225)
Watch ...	Sales D...		H5	$3.00	=H1/H3

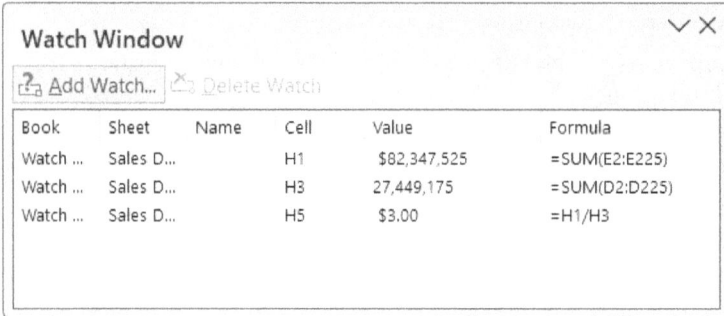

You can quickly jump to a cell that is listed in the Watch Window by double-clicking on its entry.

When you save a file containing cells that have been added to the Watch Window, these cells remain in the Watch Window next time the file is opened.

Note: If the Watch Window is not displayed you can activate it by going to the **Formulas** tab and in the **Formula Auditing** group clicking **Watch Window**.

Rather than having to remember what each cell reference refers to, it is useful to name the cells that you want to watch via the Watch Window (refer to "*Using the Name Box*" for further information on creating a named range).

Viewing Formulas

Excel includes a feature that lets you display the underlying formulas in a worksheet rather than their calculated results.

You can toggle this view by pressing **CTRL+`** (the key that also shows ~) or by selecting the **Formulas** tab on the Ribbon and from the **Formula Auditing** group, selecting the **Show Formulas** command.

If you print while this option is enabled, the formulas will appear on the printout exactly as they do on screen. This is especially useful for auditing or troubleshooting spreadsheets, particularly when row and column headings are also included (refer to "*Displaying Row and Column Headings on a Printout*").

Note: The show formulas command is a "toggle" command, meaning that you use the same method to enable and disable the function.

Using Custom Views

The Custom Views feature allows you to save and quickly switch between different display and print settings for the same worksheet data. Each saved view can include:

- The current worksheet display options (such as gridlines, headings, and zoom level).

- Hidden or visible rows and columns.

- The current print settings (such as print area, margins, page orientation, and headers/footers).

This feature is useful when you want to create different perspectives of the same data, for example, a detailed view for analysis and a summarised view for presentation or printing.

The following steps describe how to use the Custom Views feature.

1) Ensure that you have the desired settings (ie: view settings, hidden rows and columns) in effect.

2) Go to the **View** tab on the Ribbon and from the **Workbook Views** group, click **Custom Views**.

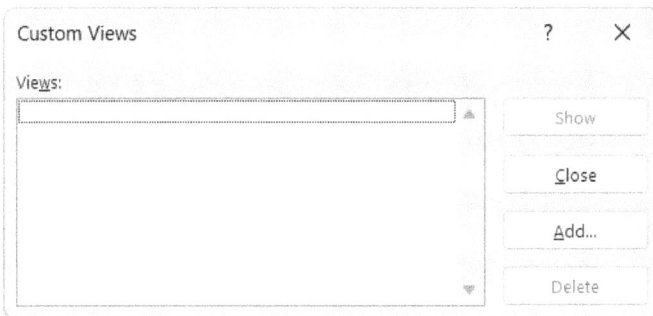

3) Click **Add**, enter a name for the view, and select whether to include: **Print settings** and/or **Hidden rows, columns, and filter settings**.

4) Click **OK** to save the view.

To switch between views, go to the **View** tab on the Ribbon and from the **Workbook Views** group, click **Custom Views**. Select the view that you want to display and click the **Show** button.

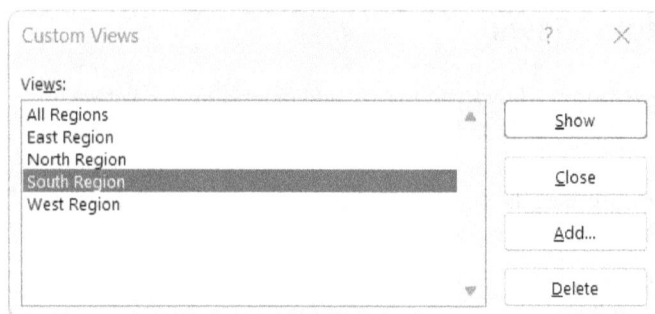

Note: It is useful to create a view for the current (or default) view, as there is no way to un-apply a view that you "show" – you can only show another view.

To speed up the process of switching between views, add the **Custom Views** button (located in the **All command** category of the "Customize Quick Access" dialog box) to the Quick Access area on the Excel Title Bar. Refer to "*Customising the Quick Access Toolbar*" for further information.

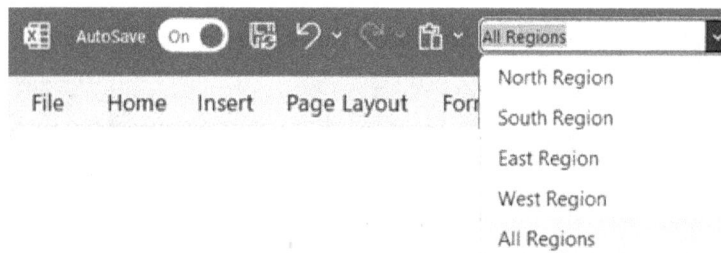

You can also create a new view by typing the view name into the "Custom Views" drop-down box.

Checking Formulas for Errors

Excel's error checking feature checks your spreadsheet for errors (eg: formulas with error values, divide by zero errors, numbers stored as text, formulas referring to empty cells, etc.), and flags cells with errors with a green indicator in the upper left corner of the cell.

When you select a cell flagged as having an error, the **Error Indicator button** appears next to the cell. You can click the drop-down arrow next to this error indicator button to get further information on the error, show the calculation steps for the formula, or ignore the error.

Error indicator flag in top left of cell

Error Indicator button

Error checking options

You can disable automatic error checking if required.

1) Select the **File** tab on the Ribbon and then select the **Options** command.

2) Click on **Formulas** category.

3) From the **Error Checking** section, disable the **Enable background error checking** option.

4) If required, you can elect to customise error checking options, such as the **Indicate Errors Using this color** and the **Error checking rules**.

5) Click **OK** to apply the change.

Note: You can activate the error checking feature via the **Formulas** tab on the Ribbon. The **Error Checking** command allows you to investigate errors on the current sheet.

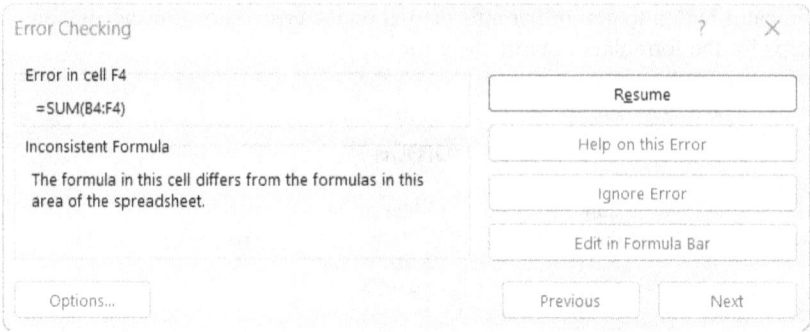

Tracing Cell Relationships

Excel includes a set of Formula Auditing tools that help you visually trace relationships between cells. These tools allow you to:

- Identify **precedent** cells – cells that provide data to the selected cell's formula.

- Identify **dependent** cells – cells that rely on the selected cell's value or formula.

To trace precedents:

1) Click on a cell containing a formula.

2) Go to the **Formulas** tab on the Ribbon.

3) In the **Formula Auditing** group, click **Trace Precedents**. Excel draws blue arrows from each cell that influences the selected formula. Clicking **Trace Precedents** multiple times expands the trace to show additional levels of linked cells.

4) Use the **Remove Arrows** button to clear the precedent arrows from the spreadsheet.

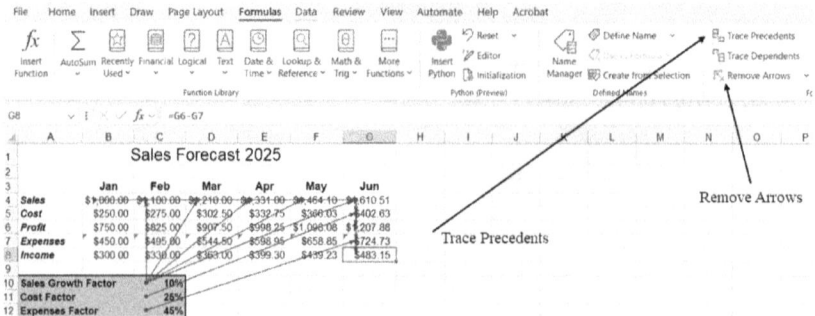

To trace dependents:

1) Click on the cell whose value is used in other formulas (this can be a constant value or a cell containing a formula).

2) Go to the **Formulas** tab on the Ribbon.

3) In the **Formula Auditing** group, click **Trace Dependents**. Excel draws blue arrows pointing to all cells that depend on the selected cell's value. Clicking **Trace Dependents** multiple times shows additional levels of dependent cells throughout the workbook.

4) Use the **Remove Arrows** button to clear the dependent arrows from the spreadsheet.

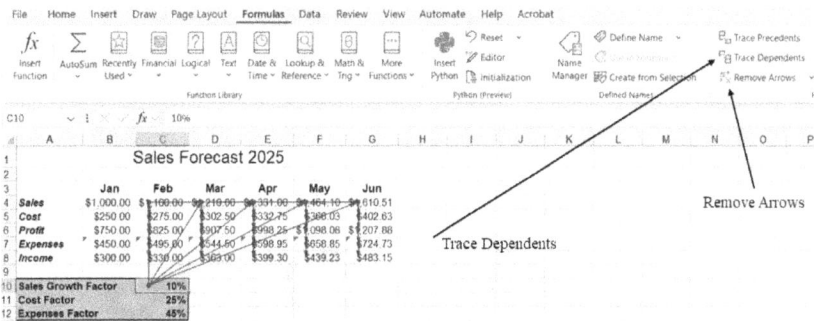

When trace arrows are displayed, look for:

- Blue dots at the end of trace lines – these indicate referenced cells.

- Arrowheads pointing towards dependent or precedent cells.

You can double-click a blue dot to move directly to the next cell referenced in the trace. Double-clicking an arrowhead navigates backwards through the chain of traced cells.

If the traced cell is on another worksheet, Excel will display a **Go To** dialog box, allowing you to jump directly to that sheet and cell.

Note: If you print the spreadsheet with the trace lines and arrows displayed, the lines and arrows will be printed with the spreadsheet.

FORMATTING

Format Part of a Cell

You can apply formatting to just part of the text inside a cell.

Simply edit the cell, highlight the portion of text you want to change, and then apply formatting such as bold, italic, underline, font size, or colour from the **Home** tab on the Ribbon.

This is a useful way to emphasise key words in labels, titles, or notes without affecting the entire cell.

Best Fit Column Widths

To quickly adjust the width of a column to accommodate the widest entry, position the mouse pointer in the grooved area between the column headings and double-click.

Double-click here to
adjust column width to
the widest entry

	A	B	
1		**2023**	
2	Adelaide,	446,838	8
3	Albany, W:	342,656	5
4	Alice Sprir	825,908	3

If multiple columns are selected, double-clicking between any two column headings will adjust all columns in the selection so that they are as wide as the longest entry in their respective columns.

Changing the Standard Column Width

You can change the default column width for all columns in a worksheet using the following steps:

1) Select the **Home** tab on the Ribbon and in the **Cells** group, click the drop-down arrow next to **Format**.

2) Select **Default Width** from the drop-down menu.

3) Enter the desired column width and click **OK**.

Standard Width	?	✕
Standard column width:	8.11	
	OK	Cancel

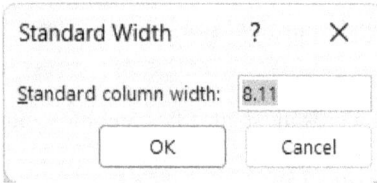

Note: This sets the standard width for all columns in the current worksheet. If you have previously adjusted the width of a column, changing the standard width will not affect it (ie: the width remains as you set it).

Copying Ranges with Column Widths

When you copy a range of cells to another location, Excel does not automatically copy the column widths. The following steps describe how to copy the column widths of the source data to the destination area.

1) Copy the desired range of cells to the clipboard.

2) Move to the destination and select the starting cell where you want to apply the formatting.

3) On the **Home** tab, in the **Clipboard** group, click the drop-down arrow under **Paste**, then choose the **Keep Source Column Widths** option.

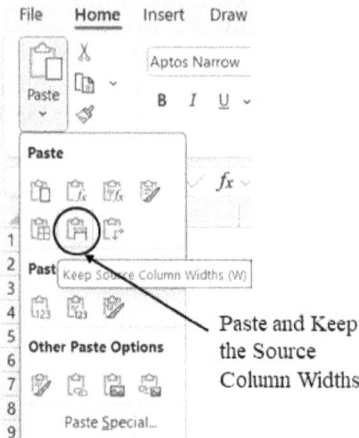

Paste and Keep the Source Column Widths

Using the Format Painter

The Format Painter allows you to copy the formatting of a cell or range to other areas of the worksheet. Formatting includes features such as number formats, borders, fill colours, fonts, and alignment.

1) Select the cell or range that contains the formatting you want to copy.

2) On the **Home** tab, in the **Clipboard** group, click the **Format Painter** button. As your mouse pointer moves back to the worksheet, it will appear as a paintbrush symbol.

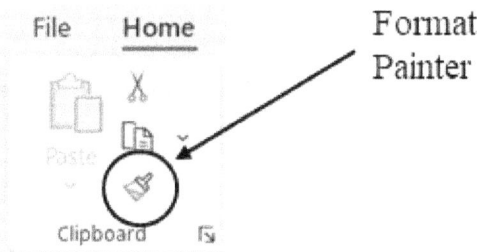

3) Click on the cell (or click and drag over the range of cells) to apply the copied formatting.

This is a great technique to use when a new column is added to the spreadsheet and you want to format it in the same way as other columns in the spreadsheet. Select all the cells that constitute the format for one column and use the format painter to copy these to the new column.

Note: If you double-click the format painter button, the feature enables you to continue copying the selected format to multiple ranges (ie: the paintbrush pointer remains after you finish copying to the first cell or range). Once you have finished working with the format painter, press **ESC** (or click the format painter button again).

Hiding Cell Contents

Excel allows you to hide many elements – columns, rows, sheets, and even entire workbooks. However, there is no specific command to hide an individual cell.

A workaround is to use a custom number format. Number formats in Excel can contain up to four sections, each separated by a semicolon (;), in the order:

Positive ; Negative ; Zero ; Text

By applying the custom number format ;;; (three semicolons), Excel is instructed to display nothing for any type of value, effectively making the cell appear hidden without deleting its contents.

In the following example, column E contains salary figures. Rather than hide the entire column, we want to hide the values contained in cells E3 and E9, the two employees in the "Management" department.

	A	B	C	D	E
1	Employee Code	First Name	Surname	Department	Salary
2	D3872	Ingrid	Wheeler	SALES	$76,791
3	C4875	Ryan	Nelson	MANAGEMENT	$162,750
4	C7209	David	Garvey	SALES	$98,499
5	C7544	Travis	Edwards	MANUFACTURING	$107,700
6	D2622	Arjun	Mehra	SALES	$85,000
7	B9615	Tim	Mielnik	ADMINISTRATION	$67,000
8	A5235	Lyn	Daniels	ADMINISTRATION	$83,100
9	D1510	Layla	Al-Farouqi	MANAGEMENT	$92,070
10	B7335	Kirstie	Small	MANUFACTURING	$117,400
11	A6508	Robyn	Ohlsen	ADMINISTRATION	$85,400

The following steps describe how to hide cell contents on the worksheet.

1) Select the cells that you want to hide (in this example cells E3 and E9).

2) Right-click over the selected cell or range and choose the **Format Cells** command.

3) Click on the **Number** tab if necessary, and then select the **Custom** category.

4) Enter the code ;;; in the **Type** field, as shown below.

Format Cells   ? ✕

Number   Alignment   Font   Border   Fill   Protection

Category:

General	Sample
Number	
Currency	
Accounting	Type:
Date	...
Time	
Percentage	h:mm:ss
Fraction	d/mm/yyyy h:mm
Scientific	mm:ss
Text	mm:ss.0
Special	@
Custom	[h]:mm:ss

_-$* #,##0_-;-$* #,##0_-;_-$* "-"_-;_-@_-
_-* #,##0_-;-* #,##0_-;_-* "-"_-;_-@_-
_-$* #,##0.00_-;-$* #,##0.00_-;_-$* "-"??_-;_-@_-
_-* #,##0.00_-;-* #,##0.00_-;_-* "-"??_-;_-@_-
_($* #,##0.00_);_($* (#,##0.00);_($* "-"??_);_(@_)
$#,##0

Delete

Type the number format code, using one of the existing codes as a starting point.

OK   Cancel

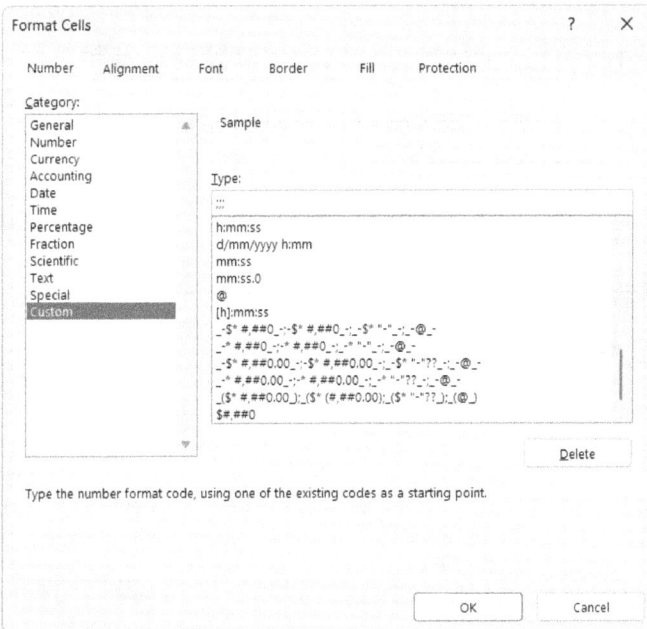

5) Click **OK** to apply the format.

Notice that the cell results are hidden, however when either cell is selected you can still see the contents of the cells in the formula bar. The following steps describe how to remove the cell contents from the formula bar by protecting the worksheet.

1) Select the cells that you want to hide (in this example cells E3 and E9) and ensure they have the custom number format **;;;** applied (refer to previous steps).

2) Right-click over the selected cell or range and choose the **Format Cells** command.

3) Click on the **Protection** tab, enable the **Hidden** option and click **OK**.

4) On the **Review** tab, in the **Protect** group, click **Protect Sheet** button. Adjust the protection options if required (you can also specify a password if desired).

5) Click **OK** to apply protection to the worksheet. The cells will be hidden, both on the worksheet and in the formula bar.

Quick Borders

To quickly add a border around a group of selected cells you can use the keyboard shortcut **CTRL+SHIFT+&**.

To remove any border lines from a group of selected cells you can use the keyboard shortcut **CTRL+SHIFT+minus sign**.

Drawing Borders

You can quickly add borders to cells by drawing them directly onto the worksheet.

1)   On the **Home** tab, in the **Font** group, click the arrow next to the **Borders** button and select **Draw Border**. The mouse pointer will change to a pencil icon, and the **Draw Outside Borders** tool will appear on the Ribbon.

2)   Click on the drop-down arrow next to the **Draw Outside Borders** tool and then from the **Line Style** drop-down list, choose the style of border you want to apply.

3)   Click on the drop-down arrow next to the **Draw Outside Borders** tool and then from the **Line Color** drop-down list, select the desired border colour.

4)   Click and drag across the cells where you want to apply the border. Excel will draw the border as you move the mouse.

5)   Press the **Esc** key to exit the Draw Border mode.

Note: The default border that is drawn is an outline (ie: lines are placed on the outside of the selected area only). To place a border around every cell in the area you select, select the **Draw Border Grid** option at Step 1.

You can clear the border formatting from a range of cells by selecting the **Erase Border** option from the **Borders** button. The mouse pointer will change shape to an eraser, which you can use to select the cells from which you want to remove the border(s).

Formatting Cells Greater or Less Than a Specific Value

Excel includes a powerful feature that allows you to dynamically change the formatting of individual cells based on the results displayed in that cell.

For example, you may want to show all the values over 500 in red text, or all values between 500 and 1000 with yellow shading.

In the following example, values that are over 65,000 are to be formatted with a yellow background and dark yellow text. Values under 30,000 are to be formatted with blue text that is double-underlined.

	A	B	C	D	E
1		QTR 1	QTR 2	QTR 3	QTR 4
2	BRICKLAYERS	46,304	49,774	29,912	65,389
3	TILERS	52,588	59,717	68,923	71,495
4	PAINTERS	62,561	69,735	70,907	59,408
5	LANDSCAPERS	74,073	22,983	74,238	50,627
6	SUPERVISORS	95,616	57,471	56,232	82,704
7	ENGINEERS	66,117	66,578	67,948	94,888
8	CARPENTERS	46,077	57,548	42,395	28,863
9	GENERAL LABOUR	29,019	48,312	54,921	35,504

1) Select the cells that you want to apply the conditional format to (in this example cells B2 to E9).

2) Select the **Home** tab, and from the **Styles** group click **Conditional Formatting** ➔ **Highlight Cells Rules** ➔ **Greater Than** command.

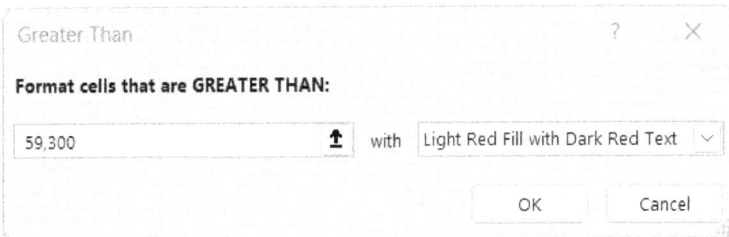

Greater Than	? X
Format cells that are GREATER THAN:	
59,300 ⬆ with Light Red Fill with Dark Red Text ⌄	
OK Cancel	

3) Enter the required value in the **Format cells that are GREATER THAN** box (in this example "65000").

4) Select the required format from the **with** drop-down list (in this example "Yellow Fill with Dark Yellow Text") and click **OK**.

5) Ensure the cells that you want to apply the conditional format to are selected (in this example cells B2 to E9).

6) Select the **Home** tab, and from the **Styles** group click **Conditional Formatting** ➔ **Highlight Cells Rules** ➔ **Less Than** command.

7) Enter the required value in the **Format cells that are LESS THAN** box (in this example "30000").

8) In this example, the format required isn't listed in the available options, so select **Custom Format** from the **with** drop-down list. The "Format Cells" dialog box is displayed, allowing you to specify the exact formatting options you want when the condition is met (in this case blue **Color** and double **Underline** can be selected from the **Font** tab).

9) Click **OK** twice to confirm the selected formatting options and return to the worksheet. The results of the conditional formatting will be displayed (as shown below). The conditional formats will be adjusted as the values in the spreadsheet change.

	A	B	C	D	E
1		QTR 1	QTR 2	QTR 3	QTR 4
2	BRICKLAYERS	46,304	49,774	29,912	65,389
3	TILERS	52,588	59,717	68,923	71,495
4	PAINTERS	62,561	69,735	70,907	59,408
5	LANDSCAPERS	74,073	22,983	74,238	50,627
6	SUPERVISORS	95,616	57,471	56,232	82,704
7	ENGINEERS	66,117	66,578	67,948	94,888
8	CARPENTERS	46,077	57,548	42,395	28,863
9	GENERAL LABOUR	29,019	48,312	54,921	35,504

Conditionally Formatting Top Percentages

Excel's Conditional Formatting feature allows you to highlight cells automatically based on their relative ranking in a range.

In the following example, the top 25% of calls taken are to be formatted with a green background and bold text.

	A	B	C	D	E	F	G
1	Agent	Team	Start Time	Finish Time	Shift Length	Calls Taken	Average Call Length
2	Aaliyah	Connection Crew	8:00 AM	4:30 PM	8.50	75	4:32
3	Amira	Connection Crew	8:30 AM	3:45 PM	7.25	52	6:23
4	Connor	Echo Squad	8:15 AM	5:45 PM	9.50	65	5:18
5	Elena	Ring Masters	8:00 AM	3:45 PM	7.75	70	4:25
6	Glenn	Ring Masters	10:00 AM	5:45 PM	7.75	99	3:36
7	Haruto	Echo Squad	8:45 AM	6:00 PM	9.25	65	6:29
8	Isabella	Echo Squad	9:30 AM	4:15 PM	6.75	58	5:24
9	Janet	Connection Crew	9:00 AM	3:30 PM	6.50	37	6:44
10	Kwame	Ring Masters	9:30 AM	4:45 PM	7.25	59	4:41
11	Luca	Echo Squad	8:45 AM	4:45 PM	8.00	75	3:56
12	Omar	Echo Squad	9:30 AM	3:45 PM	6.25	53	5:01
13	Rajesh	Connection Crew	10:15 AM	4:30 PM	6.25	32	6:56
14	Shivali	Ring Masters	9:45 AM	5:30 PM	7.75	83	4:01
15	Sophia	Ring Masters	8:15 AM	5:30 PM	9.25	93	4:45
16	Tariq	Echo Squad	10:15 AM	4:45 PM	6.50	43	5:57
17	Warwick	Ring Masters	8:15 AM	3:30 PM	7.25	46	6:19
18	Yuki	Echo Squad	9:00 AM	3:45 PM	6.75	56	4:29

1) Select the cells that you want to apply the conditional format to (in this example F2 to F18).

2) Select the **Home** tab and from the **Styles** group click **Conditional Formatting ➜ Top/Bottom Rules ➜ Top 10%** command.

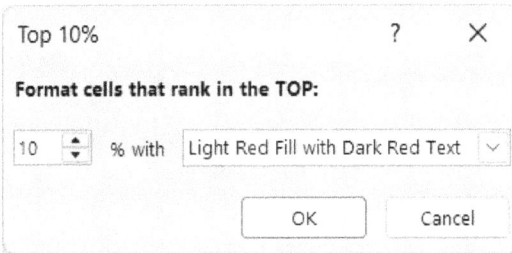

Top 10%   ? ✕

Format cells that rank in the TOP:

| 10 ⏶⏷ | % with | Light Red Fill with Dark Red Text ⌄ |

    OK   Cancel

---

3) In the dialog box, replace "10" with **25** to highlight the top 25% of values.

4) From the **with** drop-down list select **Custom Format**. The "Format Cells" dialog box will be displayed.

5) On the **Fill** tab, choose a green background colour.

6) On the **Font** tab, select **Bold**.

7) Click **OK** twice to confirm the formatting and return to the worksheet.

The spreadsheet will now display the top 25% of values in green with bold text, and the formatting will automatically adjust as the data changes.

Formatting

	A	B	C	D	E	F	G
1	Agent	Team	Start Time	Finish Time	Shift Length	Calls Taken	Average Call Length
2	Aaliyah	Connection Crew	8:00 AM	4:30 PM	8.50	75	4:32
3	Amira	Connection Crew	8:30 AM	3:45 PM	7.25	52	6:23
4	Connor	Echo Squad	8:15 AM	5:45 PM	9.50	65	5:18
5	Elena	Ring Masters	8:00 AM	3:45 PM	7.75	70	4:25
6	Glenn	Ring Masters	10:00 AM	5:45 PM	7.75	99	3:36
7	Haruto	Echo Squad	8:45 AM	6:00 PM	9.25	65	6:29
8	Isabella	Echo Squad	9:30 AM	4:15 PM	6.75	58	5:24
9	Janet	Connection Crew	9:00 AM	3:30 PM	6.50	37	6:44
10	Kwame	Ring Masters	9:30 AM	4:45 PM	7.25	59	4:41
11	Luca	Echo Squad	8:45 AM	4:45 PM	8.00	75	3:56
12	Omar	Echo Squad	9:30 AM	3:45 PM	6.25	53	5:01
13	Rajesh	Connection Crew	10:15 AM	4:30 PM	6.25	32	6:56
14	Shivali	Ring Masters	9:45 AM	5:30 PM	7.75	83	4:01
15	Sophia	Ring Masters	8:15 AM	5:30 PM	9.25	93	4:45
16	Tariq	Echo Squad	10:15 AM	4:45 PM	6.50	43	5:57
17	Warwick	Ring Masters	8:15 AM	3:30 PM	7.25	46	6:19
18	Yuki	Echo Squad	9:00 AM	3:45 PM	6.75	56	4:29

Using Icon Sets to Highlight Performance

Excel's **Icon Sets** (part of Conditional Formatting) let you quickly visualise data by adding symbols such as arrows, traffic lights, or flags beside your values. They're especially useful for spotting patterns at a glance, for example highlighting projects that are ahead of schedule, showing departments with the highest customer satisfaction, or comparing regions with the lowest costs.

By customising the rule, you can decide what each icon means and even reverse the order so that lower numbers are flagged as good and higher numbers as poor.

In the following example, the shortest call durations will be shown with a green flag, medium with a yellow flag, and the longest with a red flag.

	A	B	C	D	E	F	G
1	Agent	Team	Start Time	Finish Time	Shift Length	Calls Taken	Average Call Length
2	Aaliyah	Connection Crew	8:00 AM	4:30 PM	8.50	75	4:32
3	Amira	Connection Crew	8:30 AM	3:45 PM	7.25	52	6:23
4	Connor	Echo Squad	8:15 AM	5:45 PM	9.50	65	5:18
5	Elena	Ring Masters	8:00 AM	3:45 PM	7.75	70	4:25
6	Glenn	Ring Masters	10:00 AM	5:45 PM	7.75	99	3:36
7	Haruto	Echo Squad	8:45 AM	6:00 PM	9.25	65	6:29
8	Isabella	Echo Squad	9:30 AM	4:15 PM	6.75	58	5:24
9	Janet	Connection Crew	9:00 AM	3:30 PM	6.50	37	6:44
10	Kwame	Ring Masters	9:30 AM	4:45 PM	7.25	59	4:41
11	Luca	Echo Squad	8:45 AM	4:45 PM	8.00	75	3:56
12	Omar	Echo Squad	9:30 AM	3:45 PM	6.25	53	5:01
13	Rajesh	Connection Crew	10:15 AM	4:30 PM	6.25	32	6:56
14	Shivali	Ring Masters	9:45 AM	5:30 PM	7.75	83	4:01
15	Sophia	Ring Masters	8:15 AM	5:30 PM	9.25	93	4:45
16	Tariq	Echo Squad	10:15 AM	4:45 PM	6.50	43	5:57
17	Warwick	Ring Masters	8:15 AM	3:30 PM	7.25	46	6:19
18	Yuki	Echo Squad	9:00 AM	3:45 PM	6.75	56	4:29

1) Select the cells that you want to apply the conditional format to (in this example cells G2 to G18).

2) Select the **Home** tab and from the **Styles** group click **Conditional Formatting → Icon Sets** and then select the **3 Flags** set of icons.

3) With the cells still selected click on the **Conditional Formatting** button and select the **Manage Rules** command. The "Conditional Formatting Rules Manager" dialog box will be displayed.

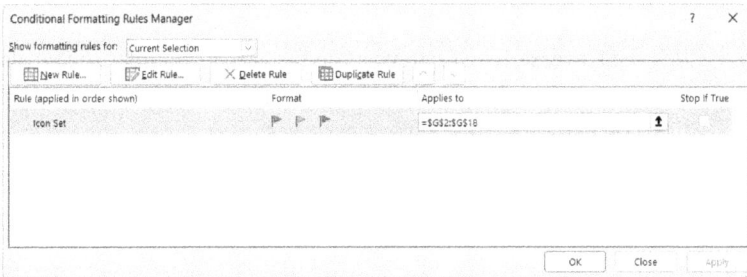

4) Ensure the rule that you just applied is highlighted and click the **Edit Rule** button. The "Edit Formatting Rule" dialog box will be displayed.

5) Click the **Reverse Icon Order** button to reverse the order so that shorter times show green, medium show yellow, and longer times show red.

6) Click **OK** twice to return to the worksheet.

The worksheet will now display flags beside each call length, making it easy to identify the agents with the fastest call handling times.

	A	B	C	D	E	F	G
1	Agent	Team	Start Time	Finish Time	Shift Length	Calls Taken	Average Call Length
2	Aaliyah	Connection Crew	8:00 AM	4:30 PM	8.50	75	⏴ 4:32
3	Amira	Connection Crew	8:30 AM	3:45 PM	7.25	52	⏴ 6:23
4	Connor	Echo Squad	8:15 AM	5:45 PM	9.50	65	⏴ 5:18
5	Elena	Ring Masters	8:00 AM	3:45 PM	7.75	70	⏴ 4:25
6	Glenn	Ring Masters	10:00 AM	5:45 PM	7.75	99	⏴ 3:36
7	Haruto	Echo Squad	8:45 AM	6:00 PM	9.25	65	⏴ 6:29
8	Isabella	Echo Squad	9:30 AM	4:15 PM	6.75	58	⏴ 5:24
9	Janet	Connection Crew	9:00 AM	3:30 PM	6.50	37	⏴ 6:44
10	Kwame	Ring Masters	9:30 AM	4:45 PM	7.25	59	⏴ 4:41
11	Luca	Echo Squad	8:45 AM	4:45 PM	8.00	75	⏴ 3:56
12	Omar	Echo Squad	9:30 AM	3:45 PM	6.25	53	⏴ 5:01
13	Rajesh	Connection Crew	10:15 AM	4:30 PM	6.25	32	⏴ 6:56
14	Shivali	Ring Masters	9:45 AM	5:30 PM	7.75	83	⏴ 4:01
15	Sophia	Ring Masters	8:15 AM	5:30 PM	9.25	93	⏴ 4:45
16	Tariq	Echo Squad	10:15 AM	4:45 PM	6.50	43	⏴ 5:57
17	Warwick	Ring Masters	8:15 AM	3:30 PM	7.25	46	⏴ 6:19
18	Yuki	Echo Squad	9:00 AM	3:45 PM	6.75	56	⏴ 4:29

Creating Mini Bar Charts Inside Cells

The **Data Bars** Conditional Formatting option provides a quick way to visualise numbers by shading each cell with a bar that reflects its value relative to the others.

Larger numbers show longer bars, smaller numbers show shorter bars. This makes it easy to compare values side by side without creating a separate chart, such as spotting who made the most sales, which products sold best, or where costs were lowest.

In the following example, data bars are added to the column containing the profit figures.

	A	B	C	D
1		AUSTRALIA - COMBINED TOTALS		
2	Month	Sales ($AUD)	Profit Margin	Profit ($AUD)
3	January	2,496,000	20.2%	505,310
4	February	2,851,000	21.1%	602,520
5	March	2,904,000	20.2%	585,520
6	April	3,016,000	24.1%	727,580
7	May	2,366,000	26.3%	622,700
8	June	2,177,000	24.3%	528,040
9	July	2,428,000	16.5%	399,860
10	August	2,290,000	20.6%	471,780
11	September	2,654,000	21.2%	561,440
12	October	3,199,000	19.8%	634,750
13	November	2,533,000	20.5%	518,970
14	December	3,059,000	22.6%	690,180
15				
16	TOTAL	31,973,000	21.4%	6,848,650

1) Select the cells that you want to apply the conditional format to (in this example cells D3 to D14).

2) Select the **Home** tab and from the **Styles** group click **Conditional Formatting ➜ Data Bars** and then select one of the **Gradient Fill or Solid Fill** options.

	A	B	C	D
1		AUSTRALIA - COMBINED TOTALS		
2	Month	Sales ($AUD)	Profit Margin	Profit ($AUD)
3	January	2,496,000	20.2%	505,310
4	February	2,851,000	21.1%	602,520
5	March	2,904,000	20.2%	585,520
6	April	3,016,000	24.1%	727,580
7	May	2,366,000	26.3%	622,700
8	June	2,177,000	24.3%	528,040
9	July	2,428,000	16.5%	399,860
10	August	2,290,000	20.6%	471,780
11	September	2,654,000	21.2%	561,440
12	October	3,199,000	19.8%	634,750
13	November	2,533,000	20.5%	518,970
14	December	3,059,000	22.6%	690,180
15				
16	TOTAL	31,973,000	21.4%	6,848,650

Highlight Cells Containing Specific Text

Conditional Formatting makes it easy to visually flag cells that contain certain words or phrases.

For example, in the list below, you may want to highlight all Overdue tasks in the "Status" column.

	A	B	C	D	E
1	Task ID	Task Name	Owner	Status	Due Date
2	101	Client Proposal Draft	Omar	Overdue	20/01/2025
3	102	Cloud Migration	Rachel	Overdue	25/07/2025
4	103	Compliance Audit	Wei	Overdue	1/07/2025
5	104	Budget Review	Ian	Pending	28/02/2025
6	105	Quarterly Town Hall	Laura	In Progress	15/08/2025
7	106	Supplier Contract Renewal	Omar	Pending	20/03/2025
8	107	Customer Onboarding Pack	Aiko	Completed	5/08/2025
9	108	Social Media Campaign	Aiko	In Progress	15/05/2025

1) Select the range you want to check (i.e. the cells in column D in this example).

2) Select the **Home** tab on the Ribbon, and from the Styles group, click on the **Conditional Formatting** button and select **New Rule**. The "New Formatting Rule" dialog box will be displayed.

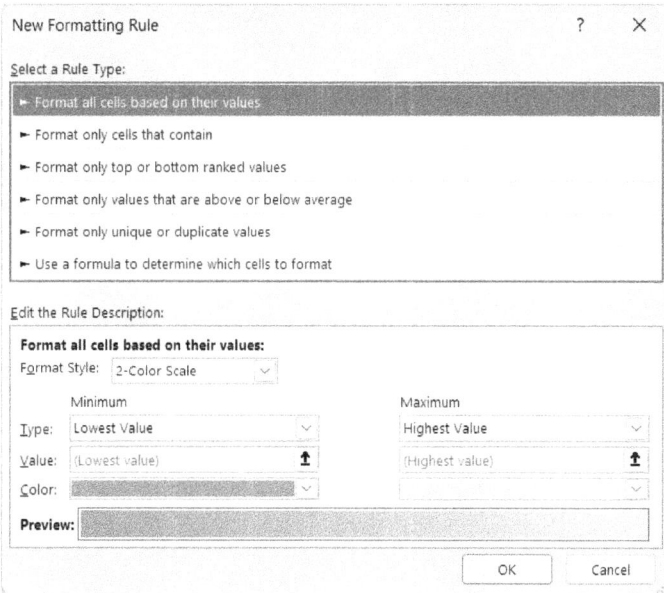

3) Select the **Use a formula to determine which cells to format** option.

4) Enter a formula to search for the text you want to highlight, with the cell reference matching the top-left cell of the range you selected in step 1, for example:
=SEARCH("Overdue",D2)
which finds the word "Overdue" anywhere in column D.

5) Click the **Format** button. The "Format Cells" dialog box will be displayed, allowing you to choose the formatting you want in order for the cells to stand out (e.g., bold red text or a fill colour).

6) Click **OK** twice to apply. Every task with the status "Overdue" will be highlighted automatically.

Automatically Add Lines Between Groups

You can use Conditional Formatting to automatically draw a line between sections in your data when the value in a key column changes (e.g. Department, Location, Consultant, Date, etc.).

In the following example, a horizontal line is added above the first row of each new Region.

	A	B	C	D
1	**Sales Rep**	**ID**	**Region**	**Sales**
2	Arjun	302	West	12,750.00
3	Ava	310	South	16,100.00
4	Chen	313	West	10,200.00
5	Ethan	312	North	9,700.00
6	Grace	304	West	13,300.00
7	Hannah	317	East	14,950.00
8	Isabella	306	West	14,100.00
9	Leila	303	Central	13,950.00
10	Liam	311	North	14,350.00
11	Lucas	316	South	12,400.00
12	Marcus	307	Central	15,100.00
13	Maya	315	East	15,200.00
14	Noah	301	South	11,300.00
15	Oliver	309	East	13,700.00
16	Owen	308	Central	11,950.00
17	Sofia	314	North	12,800.00
18	Zara	305	Central	14,400.00

1) Sort the data by the column that you want the items grouped by (in this example, column C).

2) Select the range containing the data, without the headings (in this example A2:D18).

3) Select the **Home** tab on the Ribbon, and from the Styles group, click on the **Conditional Formatting** button and select **New Rule**. The "New Formatting Rule" dialog box will be displayed.

4) Select the **Use a formula to determine which cells to format** option.

5) Enter a formula that compares the current row's value to the one above it. For this example, the Region column is C, so the formula would be: **=AND($C2<>$C1, ROW()>ROW($A$2))**

6) Click the **Format** button and from the "Format Cells" dialog box click on the **Border** tab.

7) Add a top border, and choose a style/colour.

8) Click **OK** twice to return to the worksheet.

Copying Conditional Formats to Other Cells

You can copy conditional formats to other cells. Select the cells that have the conditional formats you want to copy, click the **Format Painter** button, and then select the cells that you want the same conditional formats to apply to.

This action copies all formatting attributes (including conditional formats). Refer to "*Using the Format Painter*" for further information on copying spreadsheet formatting.

Automatic List Formatting

You can make the creation of lists in Excel easier by enabling the **Extend data range formats and formulas** feature. When Excel detects a formatting or formula pattern in a list, it will automatically apply that pattern to new cells added to the list. This saves you from having to manually format or reapply formulas for each new entry.

1) Select the **File** tab on the Ribbon and then select the **Options** command.

2) Click on the **Advanced** category.

3) Scroll down to the **Editing options** section and enable the **Extend data range formats and formulas** and click **OK**.

Displaying a Date as a Day of the Week

When you enter a column of dates in a worksheet, it's often helpful to see the day of the week for each date. You can do this by applying a custom number format.

1) Select the range of cells containing dates.

2) Right-click over the selected cell or range and choose the **Format Cells** command.

3) Click on the **Number** tab and select **Custom** in the "Category" list.

4) Type the format **dddd** in the **Type** text box, and click **OK**. You can use the related custom format **ddd** to display truncated day names such as Mon, Tue, etc.

To display the actual date and the day of the week, append the "day" format to the current date format (eg: the code **ddd dd/mm/yy** would display the date in the format "Sun 03/08/25").

If you do not want to change the format of cells containing dates, you can use the **TEXT** function to display the day of the week as a formula result, in another cell.

The syntax of the TEXT function is;
TEXT(value,format code)
where;
Value is the cell reference containing the data you want to format.
Format code is the numeric format code that you want to use to format the cell.

For example, =TEXT(A2, "dddd") would return the day of the week for the date entered in cell A2.

B2	⌄	⋮	✕	✓	_fx_ ⌄	=TEXT(A2,"dddd")	

◢	A	B	C	D	E
1	**Dates**				
2	3/08/2025	Sunday			
3	23/03/1979	Friday			
4	28/06/2004	Monday			
5	13/12/2006	Wednesday			
6	1/04/1999	Thursday			
7	6/02/2018	Tuesday			
8	8/10/1994	Saturday			

Another option would be to duplicate the dates in another column by use of a simple linking formula (eg: =A2 displays the value from cell A2). The first column of dates contains the original format, the second column of dates is formatted to display the day of the week.

Adding Additional Text to Cell Entries

If you are entering data into a spreadsheet that includes a common text component at the start or end (eg: a word such as "Invoice", or a code such as "S/N" etc.), Excel's custom number format may provide you with a useful shortcut.

You can add common text entries to a number format by placing the text inside quotation marks " " . The @ symbol is used in the number format to represent the actual text entered.

In the following example, column A has a format that adds two zeros to the beginning of the cell entry, eg: in cell A1 where the number 5 was entered, the number format causes it to display as 005.

Column B adds the text "PN" to the beginning of the cell entry, eg: in cell B1 where the number 7261 was entered, the number format displays it as PN7621.

In Column C the text is added to the end of the cell entry, in this case a space and the letters SZ, eg: in cell C1 where the number 143 was entered, the number format displays this as 143 SZ.

The codes used in the example were;

Column A	"00"0
Column B	"PN"0
Column C	0" SZ"

	A	B	C
1	005	PN7261	143 SZ
2	007	PN9123	19 SZ
3	009	PN919	232 SZ
4	0023	PN22	198 SZ
5	0019	PN1810	16 SZ
6	00101	PN2701	1010 SZ
7	002	PN712	386 SZ

The following steps describe how to create a custom number format.

1) Right-click over the selected cell or range and choose the **Format Cells** command.

2) Click on the **Number** tab and select **Custom** from the **Category** list.

3) Type the format required in the **Type** text box, and click **OK** (refer to examples above).

4) Underneath the **Type** heading, enter the custom number format code that you want to use and then click **OK**.

Working with Times

Excel stores and processes time values in a particular way. To use times effectively in formulas and to display them correctly, it is important to understand how Excel represents and calculates them. Consider the following timesheet example.

In this example, Column D subtracts the Start time from the Finish time (Column C minus Column B), so the hours worked each day are displayed correctly. The issue appears when calculating the total in cell D8, which uses the formula =SUM(D2:D6). Instead of showing 41.5 hours, Excel displays 17:30.

D8			fx	=SUM(D2:D6)
	A	B	C	D
1		Start	Finish	Hours
2	Monday	9:00	17:00	8:00
3	Tuesday	9:00	17:30	8:30
4	Wednesday	8:30	17:00	8:30
5	Thursday	8:00	17:00	9:00
6	Friday	9:00	16:30	7:30
7				
8	TOTAL			17:30

The problem becomes clear if you change the format of cell D8 to a number format (for example, by clicking the comma button on the toolbar). Excel then shows the result as 1.73. This is because Excel stores times as fractions of a day. For instance, midnight on 15/03/2023 is stored as 45,000, meaning 45,000 days since 1 January 1900. In this system, 1.73 represents 1.73 days, which is the same as 41.5 hours.

D8			fx	=SUM(D2:D6)
	A	B	C	D
1		Start	Finish	Hours
2	Monday	9:00	17:00	8:00
3	Tuesday	9:00	17:30	8:30
4	Wednesday	8:30	17:00	8:30
5	Thursday	8:00	17:00	9:00
6	Friday	9:00	16:30	7:30
7				
8	TOTAL			1.73

To fix the issue, simply change the format of cell D8 to display a number or a custom time format that shows hours correctly.

1) Right-click over the selected cell or range and choose the **Format Cells** command.

2) Click on the **Number** tab and select **Custom** from the **Category** list.

3) Delete the current number format shown in the **Type** box.

4) Enter **[h]:mm** in the **Type** box and click **OK** to return to the worksheet.

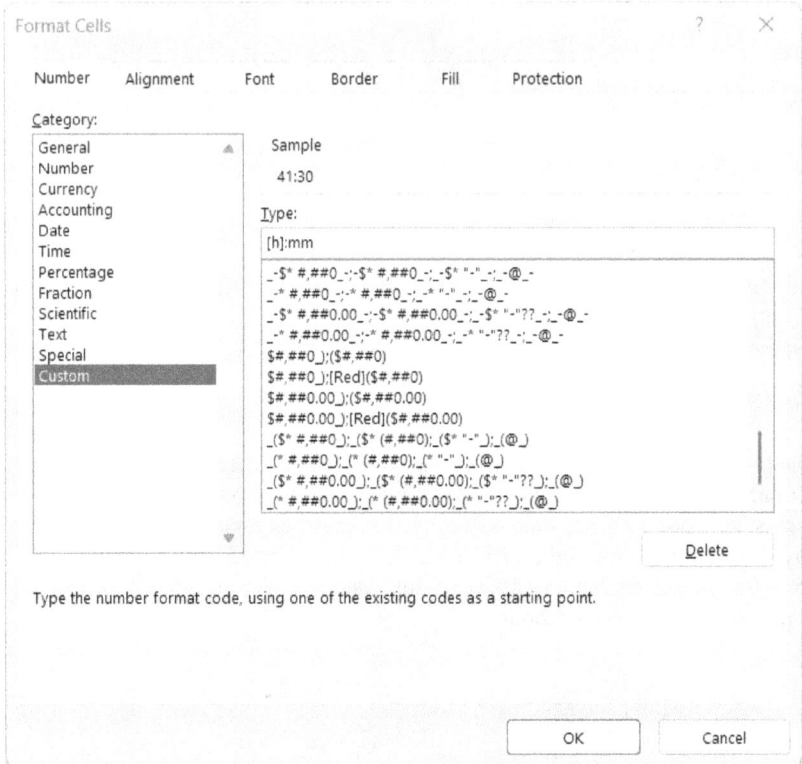

Format Cells							? ✕

Number   Alignment   Font   Border   Fill   Protection

Category:

General		Sample
Number		41:30
Currency		
Accounting		Type:
Date		[h]:mm
Time		
Percentage		_-$* #,##0_-;-$* #,##0_-;_-$* "-"_-;_-@_-
Fraction		_-* #,##0_-;-* #,##0_-;_-* "-"_-;_-@_-
Scientific		_-$* #,##0.00_-;-$* #,##0.00_-;_-$* "-"??_-;_-@_-
Text		_-* #,##0.00_-;-* #,##0.00_-;_-* "-"??_-;_-@_-
Special		$#,##0_);($#,##0)
Custom		$#,##0_);[Red]($#,##0)
		$#,##0.00_);($#,##0.00)
		$#,##0.00_);[Red]($#,##0.00)
		_($* #,##0_);_($* (#,##0);_($* "-"_);_(@_)
		_(* #,##0_);_(* (#,##0);_(* "-"_);_(@_)
		_($* #,##0.00_);_($* (#,##0.00);_($* "-"??_);_(@_)
		_(* #,##0.00_);_(* (#,##0.00);_(* "-"??_);_(@_)

Delete

Type the number format code, using one of the existing codes as a starting point.

OK   Cancel

The use of the square brackets [ ] in the number format code changes the format to elapsed time, instead of attempting to display an absolute time.

Using calculated time values in formulas presents a similar set of problems. In the following diagram, column D is multiplied by the employee's wage ($25/hour). The answer in cell E2 should be $200, but Excel calculates the answer as 8:00.

E2	⌄ ⋮ ✕ ✓ *fx* ⌄	=D2*25

◢	A	B	C	D	E
1		Start	Stop	Hours	Pay
2	Monday	9:00	17:00	8:00	8:00
3	Tuesday	9:00	17:30	8:30	20:30
4	Wednesday	8:30	17:00	8:30	20:30
5	Thursday	8:00	17:00	9:00	9:00
6	Friday	9:00	16:30	7:30	19:30
7					
8	TOTAL			41:30	

Formatting the cells with a dollar sign improves the format of the numbers, but does not display the correct results.

E2	⌄ ⋮ ✕ ✓ *fx* ⌄	=D2*25

◢	A	B	C	D	E
1		Start	Stop	Hours	Pay
2	Monday	9:00	17:00	8:00	$ 8.33
3	Tuesday	9:00	17:30	8:30	$ 8.85
4	Wednesday	8:30	17:00	8:30	$ 8.85
5	Thursday	8:00	17:00	9:00	$ 9.38
6	Friday	9:00	16:30	7:30	$ 7.81
7					
8	TOTAL			41:30	

This occurs because Excel is calculating the hours as a fraction (part) of a day. The calculation in E2 takes 8/24 hours (ie: a third of a day) and multiplies it by the pay rate. The solution is to multiply the result by 24. This will give you the correct daily wage for the employee.

E2	⌄ ⋮ ✕ ✓ *fx* ⌄	=D2*25*24

◢	A	B	C	D	E
1		Start	Stop	Hours	Pay
2	Monday	9:00	17:00	8:00	$ 200.00
3	Tuesday	9:00	17:30	8:30	$ 212.50
4	Wednesday	8:30	17:00	8:30	$ 212.50
5	Thursday	8:00	17:00	9:00	$ 225.00
6	Friday	9:00	16:30	7:30	$ 187.50
7					
8	TOTAL			41:30	

FORMULAS
AND
FUNCTIONS

Understanding AutoSum's Priorities

If you have used the AutoSum button (Σ) to quickly add sets of numbers, you may have noticed that its first preference is to add columns of numbers, rather than rows.

In the example below, using the AutoSum button in cells C1 and C2 provides the correct totals, however in cell C3 there are numbers above the cell pointer that can be added, so Excel adds the numbers in C1 and C2, instead of A3 and B3.

C3		$\times$ $\checkmark$ fx	=SUM(C1:C2)

	A	B	C	D	E
1	10	6	16		
2	12	7	19		
3	13	4	35		

To ensure that Excel always adds the numbers that you require, **highlight the cells that you want to add and the blank cell where you want the answer to appear. Then click on the AutoSum button.** This works when adding across a row, as well as down a column.

If you have several rows or several columns to add, you can highlight all the cells that you want to add, and all the blank cells where you want the answers to appear, and then click the AutoSum button once to create the entire set of totals. For example, to create the correct totals in column C in the above example, the following cells would be highlighted before clicking on the AutoSum button.

	A	B	C
1	10	6	
2	12	7	
3	13	4	

AutoSum Keyboard Shortcut

Instead of clicking on the AutoSum button (Σ), you can press **ALT+equal sign** to activate the AutoSum function.

AutoSum's Hidden Functions

The AutoSum button (Σ) on the **Home** tab has a small drop-down arrow next to it. This allows you to quickly apply other common functions such as Average, Count, Max, or Min, without having to type formulas manually.

Just like with AutoSum, you can click the drop-down, select the desired function, and Excel will try to guess the correct range. (Refer to *"Understanding AutoSum's Priorities"* for details on how Excel selects cells when you use this feature.)

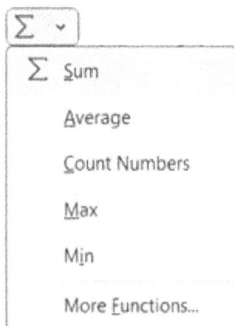

The default function of the button is always **Sum**, this will be applied unless you specifically select another function from the drop-down arrow.

AutoSum All Totals

Excel's AutoSum button can be used to quickly create both column and row totals in one action.

Highlight all the cells containing data and the cells that are to contain the totals (in this example the range to select would be cells B2 to F10 and then click the AutoSum button (Σ)).

R25	⌄	:	✕ ✓ fx ⌄			

◢	A	B	C	D	E	F
1		QTR 1	QTR 2	QTR 3	QTR 4	TOTALS
2	Cola	8,177	6,042	11,055	6,824	
3	Diet Cola	7,595	4,595	5,306	8,381	
4	Lemonade	7,494	4,953	9,015	10,708	
5	Diet Lemonade	7,227	11,801	7,557	7,857	
6	Orange	9,361	10,888	8,364	8,750	
7	Diet Orange	10,626	8,562	8,663	9,050	
8	Ginger Beer	6,393	9,840	8,605	8,718	
9	Soda Water	7,720	9,219	8,383	8,853	
10	TOTALS					

Function ScreenTips

When you enter or edit a function in Excel, you'll see a ScreenTip appear just below your formula. This provides on-the-spot guidance, showing the required arguments for that function. As you type, Excel highlights the next argument in bold, making it easier to follow the correct order.

You can also click directly on any argument name in the ScreenTip to quickly edit that part of your formula.

Additionally, if you hover your mouse pointer over the function name in the ScreenTip, it becomes a clickable hyperlink. Selecting it opens a built-in Help topic with more details and examples for that specific function.

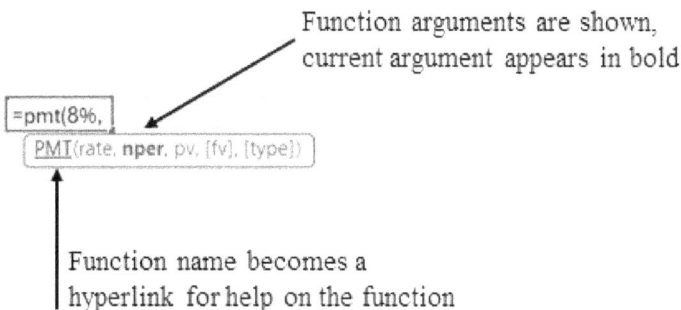

Function arguments are shown, current argument appears in bold

=pmt(8%,

PMT(rate, **nper**, pv, [fv], [type])

Function name becomes a hyperlink for help on the function

Note: If you prefer not to see these on-screen prompts, you can turn them off by selecting the **File** tab on the Ribbon and then selecting the **Options** command. In the **Advanced** category (**Display** section), disable the **Show function ScreenTips** option and click **OK** to save your changes.

Pause a Formula Without Losing It

If you're working on a complex formula and Excel refuses to accept it because of an error, you don't need to delete your work. Instead, you can pause the formula by converting it into text.

Simply remove the initial = sign. Excel will then treat the contents as plain text instead of trying to calculate it.

When you're ready to test or fix the formula, just add the = back to turn it into a working formula again.

This trick lets you keep lengthy formulas intact while you debug, without losing what you've already written.

Creating a Formula to Check Cross-Totals

In many spreadsheets, data is totaled both across rows and down columns, which often leads to the question – in the bottom-right cell, is the total derived from the column above or the row to the left?

In practice, it can be either, as both methods should produce the same result. For example, in the table below, cell E6 could be calculated as the sum of B6:D6 (row total) or as the sum of E2:E5 (column total), with both formulas returning the same grand total.

◢	A	B	C	D	E
1		January	February	March	TOTALS
2	North	17	6	10	33
3	South	5	11	7	23
4	East	16	2	18	36
5	West	12	13	12	37
6	TOTALS	50	32	47	

The IF function can be used to check that both sets of totals match in worksheets like this.

In the example shown above, the following formula can be entered in cell E6;
=IF(SUM(B6:D6)=SUM(E2:E5),SUM(B6:D6),"Error")

This formula tests whether the total of B6:D6 equals the total of E2:E5. If they match, Excel displays the sum (either total could be shown, since they are identical). If they don't match, Excel displays the message "Error".

Switching Between Relative and Absolute Referencing

When you create a formula, references to cells or ranges are usually based upon their position relative to the cell that contains the formula. When you copy a formula that uses relative references, the references in the pasted formulas update and refer to different cells *relative* to the position of the formula. For example, if you copy a formula down one row, all cell references used in that formula move down one row.

When you don't want references to change as you copy a formula to different cells, an absolute reference is used. Absolute references always refer to the same cell(s) in a formula, regardless of where the formula is copied to.

You can create an absolute reference to a cell by placing a dollar sign ($) before the parts of the reference that you do not want changed. The quickest way of entering the dollar sign is to press **F4** whilst entering (or clicking on) the cell reference in the formula.

Each time you press **F4**, Excel cycles through the different absolute and relative options available, as described in the following table.

Cell Reference	Explanation
A1	A fully relative cell.
$A$1	A fully absolute cell.
$A1	The column is made absolute, however the row is relative.
A$1	The row is made absolute, however the column is relative.

Create a Formula to Keep a Running Total

You can calculate a running (or cumulative) total in a column or row of cells by using a combination of absolute and relative references in a formula that uses the SUM function.

C2		⌄ ⋮ ✕ ✓ fx ⌄	=SUM($B$2:B2)

◢	A	B	C	[
1	Month	Units Produced	Running Total	
2	January	113,990	113,990	
3	February	169,001	282,991	
4	March	177,002	459,993	
5	April	163,194	623,187	
6	May	106,093	729,280	
7	June	80,880	810,160	
8	July	194,791	1,004,951	
9	August	141,010	1,145,961	
10	September	168,606	1,314,567	
11	October	128,457	1,443,024	
12	November	95,882	1,538,906	
13	December	194,871	1,733,777	

In the example above, a running total is kept in Column C. The following formula is entered in cell C2:
=SUM($B$2:B2)

This formula can then be copied down column C, so that each month has a running total from January to the current month.

The $B$2 (absolute reference) will be constant in each cell, while the B1 (relative reference) will be updated in each successive cell to refer to the adjacent cell in column B. Refer to "*Switching Between Relative and Absolute Referencing*" for further information on relative and absolute references.

3D Formulas

In Excel functions where you specify the start and end points of a range, the cells are separated by a colon. For instance, the following formula would return the sum of all cells in the range A1 through C4;
=SUM(A1:C4)

You can also work with ranges that extended across multiple worksheets of a workbook. For example, you may want a cell to return the sum of the values in cell A1 on the first three worksheets in your workbook.

If the worksheets are named Sheet1, Sheet2, and Sheet3, then the formula would appear as follows;
=SUM(Sheet1:Sheet3!A1)

Similarly, if you wanted the sum of all cells in the range A1 through C4 on each of the same worksheets, you could use the following formula;
=SUM(Sheet1:Sheet3!A1:C4)

These types of formulas are often described as 3D (three-dimensional) formulas. The following steps describe how to create a formula across multiple sheets.

1) Select the cell where you require the answer to the calculation.

2) Begin to enter the first part of the function you require, for example;
   =SUM(

3) Click on the **sheet tab** of the first sheet in the range that you want to use in the formula.

4) Hold down the **SHIFT** key as you click on the **sheet tab** of the last sheet in the range that you want to use in the formula.

5) Use the mouse to select the cell(s) that you want to use in the formula on whichever worksheet is currently visible.

6) Press **ENTER**.

Adding Notes to Formulas

You can add your own notes directly inside formulas, making them easier to understand later. These notes appear only in the Formula Bar when you select the cell, not in the cell itself.

Just add the N() function with a text string to the end of your formula, for example:
=SUM(B1:B23)+N("Adds the expenses for the month")

The N() function usually converts text that looks like a number into a numeric value. But if the text is non-numeric, it evaluates to zero – so it doesn't impact the calculation.

This is a useful way to keep formula explanations exactly where you need them, without cluttering your worksheet.

Smart Headings Using the IF Function

An alternative use of Excel's IF function involves altering headings depending on the current results displayed in the spreadsheet. In the following example, the heading in cell A3 is an IF function that determines whether the figure in cell B3 (the result of the formula B1-B2) is greater than or equal to zero. If it is, the heading reads "Profit", otherwise it reads "Loss".

The formula in cell A3 is;
=IF(B3>=0,"Profit","Loss")

A3	. ∨ : ✕ ✓ *fx* ∨	=IF(B3>=0,"Profit","Loss")				
	A	B	C	D	E	F
1	Income	31,747				
2	Costs	21,916				
3	Profit	9,831				

Using the IFERROR Function to Test for Errors

The IFERROR function checks a formula or expression for an error value (such as #N/A, #VALUE!, #REF!, #DIV/0!, #NUM!, #NAME?, or #NULL!) and allows you to return an alternative result if an error is found. This is useful for preventing error messages from appearing in your worksheet and instead showing something more meaningful.

For example, the formula:
=IFERROR(A1, "Error in cell")
will display "Error in cell" if cell A1 contains an error, or the value of A1 if no error exists.

The IFERROR function can also be used to handle potential errors in other calculations. In the following example, the formula entered in cell E1 checks whether the result of averaging cells D1 to D4 produces an error:
=IFERROR(AVERAGE(D1:D4), "Error in data")

If there is no error, the average is displayed.

```
=IFERROR(AVERAGE(D1:D4), "Error in data")
```

D	E	F	G	H
1979	1978			
1975				
1972				
1986				

If there is an error, the message "Error in data" appears instead.

```
=IFERROR(AVERAGE(D1:D4), "Error in data")
```

D	E	F	G	H
Jeni	Error in data			
Henry				
Jerry				
Theresa				

Note: To leave the cell blank when a formula produces an error, use a space inside the quotation marks in the IFERROR formula. For example: **=IFERROR(AVERAGE(D1:D4), " ")**

Evaluating Formulas One Expression at a Time

Even when a formula is typed correctly, Excel's evaluation order can produce an unexpected result. **Evaluate Formula** lets you step through the calculation one piece at a time so you can see exactly how Excel processes each part. It is especially useful for nested formulas and logical functions (such as IF) where multiple conditions are tested.

1) Select the cell that contains the formula you want to troubleshoot.

2) Go to the **Formulas** tab on the Ribbon, then in the **Formula Auditing** group, click **Evaluate Formula**. The "Evaluate Formula" dialog box will appear, with the first part of the formula underlined.

Evaluate Formula   ?   ✕

Reference: Evaluation:

Sheet1!$B$8   =   (B4-(B4*$B$11))-($B$12*B4)

To show the result of the underlined expression, click Evaluate. The most recent result appears italicized.

[Evaluate]   Step In   Step Out   Close

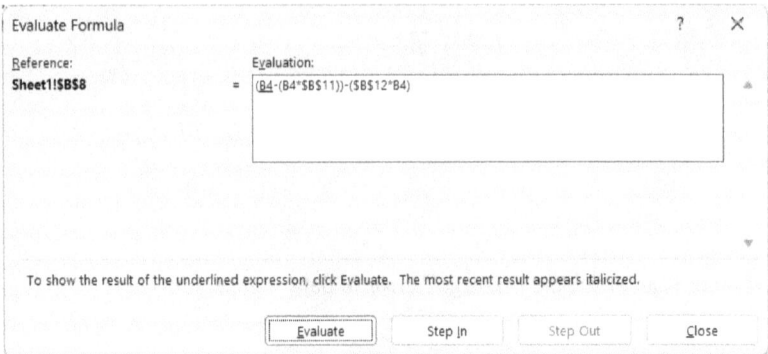

3) Click **Evaluate** to see the result of the underlined expression. If it's a cell reference, the cell's value will display. If it's another formula, Excel shows the calculated result.

4) Keep clicking **Evaluate** to move through each part of the formula step by step. When the entire formula has been processed, the button will change to **Restart**.

5) Click **Close** to return to your worksheet.

Note: When evaluating formulas, you can examine references made to cells that themselves contain formulas by using the **Step In** button. Use the **Step Out** button to return back to the main formula.

Using Range Names in Formulas

A range name is a plain English name that you assign to a cell or a range, for example you might assign the name "Jan_Sales" to the range D2:D9 containing January's sales figures (refer to *"Using the Name Box"* for further information on creating a range name).

You can use range names that you have defined when building formulas, for example: =**Units*Price** makes more sense than =**D3*D12**.

When creating a formula, press **F3** to display a list of range names that you can select from to insert into the formula.

Paste Name   ?   ✕

Paste name

Base_Pay
Hourly_Rate
OT_Hours
OT_Pay
Overtime_Factor
Total_Pay

| Paste List | OK | Cancel |

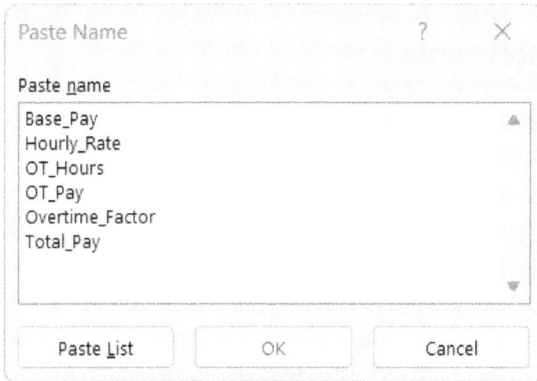

Using the AutoCalculate Feature

The AutoCalculate feature shows the result of common functions based on the cells that you highlight. This can be a useful tool for cross-checking formulas or for performing quick calculations without the need to create a formula.

1) Highlight cells that you want to use for the calculation. You can highlight non-continuous cells with this feature (refer to "*Selecting Non-Continuous Cells*" for further information on how to select non-continuous cells).

2) The AutoCalculate area, located on the right of the status bar (which is at the bottom of the screen) will display the result of the calculation (the default is to show Average, Count, and Sum).

Average: $456.78   Count: 4   Sum: $1,827.11

3) To change the functions that AutoCalculate uses, right-click over the AutoCalculate area. You can select from the functions Average, Count, Numerical Count, Minimum, Maximum, and Sum.

✓	Average	$456.78
✓	Count	4
	Numerical Count	
	Minimum	
	Maximum	
✓	Sum	$1,827.11

Streamlined IF Statements

The IFS function is a more elegant alternative to writing long, nested IF statements. It evaluates multiple conditions in order and returns the result for the first condition that is TRUE.

The syntax of the function is;
=IFS(logical_test1, value_if_true1, [logical_test2, value_if_true2], …)
where;
logical_test1 (required) is the first condition you want to test.
value_if_true1 (required) is value returned if the first condition is TRUE.
logical_test2, value_if_true2… (optional) are additional conditions and corresponding return values.

Excel checks each condition in order and as soon as it finds one that is TRUE, it returns the corresponding result. If no conditions are TRUE and no "catch-all" is provided, Excel returns a #N/A error.

In the following example, the IFS function is used to provide a rating based on the number of calls taken (greater than 100 is "Excellent", between 50 and 100 is "Good" and less than 50 is "Needs Improvement"). The formula in cell D2 is:
=IFS(C2>100,"Excellent",C2>=50,"Good",C2<50,"Needs Improvement")

D2			fx	=IFS(C2>100,"Excellent",C2>=50,"Good",C2<50,"Needs Improvement")				
	A	B	C	D	E	F	G	H	I
1	Agent	Team	Calls Taken	Rating				
2	Aaliyah	Connection Crew	57	Good				
3	Amira	Connection Crew	73	Good				
4	Connor	Echo Squad	105	Excellent				
5	Elena	Ring Masters	45	Needs Improvement				
6	Glenn	Ring Masters	106	Excellent				
7	Haruto	Echo Squad	98	Good				
8	Isabella	Echo Squad	66	Good				
9	Janet	Connection Crew	74	Good				
10	Kwame	Ring Masters	71	Good				
11	Luca	Echo Squad	37	Needs Improvement				
12	Omar	Echo Squad	89	Good				
13	Rajesh	Connection Crew	119	Excellent				
14	Shivali	Ring Masters	76	Good				
15	Sophia	Ring Masters	97	Good				
16	Tariq	Echo Squad	51	Good				
17	Warwick	Ring Masters	37	Needs Improvement				
18	Yuki	Echo Squad	95	Good				

In the following example, the IFS function is used to grade the students' test scores.

| C2 | | ✓ ⋮ ✕ ✓ fx ✓ | =IFS(B2>=90,"High Distinction",B2>=75,"Distinction",B2>=65,"Credit",B2>=50,"Pass",B2<50,"Fail") |

⊿	A	B	C	D	E	F	G	H	I	J	K	L	M	N	(
1	Student	Mark	Grade												
2	Aarav	72	Credit												
3	Angela	85	Distinction												
4	Chantell	89	Distinction												
5	Clare	89	Distinction												
6	Heather	60	Pass												
7	James	91	High Distinction												
8	Mei Ling	61	Pass												
9	Meredith	65	Credit												
10	Omar	69	Credit												
11	Patrick	81	Distinction												
12	Paul	62	Pass												
13	Priya	66	Credit												
14	Ryuichi	92	High Distinction												
15	Scott	47	Fail												
16	Trevor	63	Pass												

Generating Random Numbers

The **RAND** function allows you to create a random number in a cell. This can be useful in spreadsheets where you may require some sample data to test formulas. Because the random number function is a calculation, it can be copied to other cells where random numbers are required. A new random number is returned every time the worksheet is re-calculated. Following are some examples of the RAND function.

- The RAND function creates a random number, between 0 and 1, eg:
  0.697503, 0.78331, 0.096257;
  =RAND()

- To set a maximum value for the random number, multiply the function by the maximum value, eg: the formula below creates a random number between
  0 and 100;
  =RAND()*100

- To set a maximum and minimum value for the random number, use the formula =**RAND()*(b-a)+a**, where "a" is the minimum value and "b" is the maximum value, eg: the formula below would create a random number between 50 and 100;
  =RAND()*(100-50)+50

- To create a random number that is a whole number (by default the RAND function includes decimal places), use the formula =**INT(RAND())**, eg: the formula below would create a random whole number between 0 and 100;
  =INT(RAND()*100)

- To create a random number that is a whole number set between a maximum and minimum value, use the formula =**INT(RAND()*(b-a)+a)**,

where "a" is the minimum value and "b" is the maximum value, eg: the formula below would create a random whole number between 50 and 100;
=INT(RAND()*(100-50)+50)

Generating Random Numbers with RANDBETWEEN

The **RANDBETWEEN** function generates a random integer (whole number) between the values you specify.

The syntax of the function is;
=RANDBETWEEN(bottom,top)
where;
Bottom is the smallest number that you want returned.
Top is the largest number that you want returned.

The following formula would generate a random number between 50 and 100;
=RANDBETWEEN(50,100)

Generating Random Numbers with RANDARRAY

The RANDARRAY function fills cells with random numbers for as many rows and columns as you specify.

The syntax of the function is:
=RANDARRAY([rows],[columns],[min],[max],[integer])
where:
rows is the number of rows to fill.
columns is the number of columns to fill.
min is the minimum value to return (optional).
max is the maximum value to return (optional).
integer is TRUE for whole numbers, FALSE (or omitted) for decimals.

Following are some examples of the RANDARRAY function.

- To fill three rows and two columns with random numbers between 0 and 1 (default):
  =RANDARRAY(3,2)

A1		∨ ⋮ ✕ ✓ *fx* ∨	=RANDARRAY(3,2)		
◢	A	B	C	D	E
1	0.153846	0.46434			
2	0.401846	0.009482			
3	0.231752	0.27057			

- To generate a column of 15 random numbers:
  =RANDARRAY(15,1)

- To generate random numbers between 50 and 75 in a 3-row by 2-column block:
  =RANDARRAY(3,2,50,75)

A1		∨ ⋮ ✕ ✓ *fx* ∨	=RANDARRAY(3,2,50,75)			
◢	A	B	C	D	E	F
1	58.53287	65.4051				
2	60.46842	73.44267				
3	54.81116	63.26682				

- To generate random integers between 0 and 999 in a 5-row by 18-column block:
  =RANDARRAY(5,18,0,999,TRUE)

A1		∨ ⋮	*fx*	=RANDARRAY(5,18,0,999,TRUE)														
◢	A	B	C	D	E	F	G	H	I	J	K	L	M	N	O	P	Q	R
1	240	806	650	671	330	203	878	264	497	100	711	211	819	365	270	591	42	97
2	352	427	181	926	271	138	431	31	255	617	59	727	821	321	813	826	190	945
3	115	240	136	565	202	336	790	530	863	734	830	686	23	784	768	579	696	
4	639	204	907	663	880	756	98	470	319	916	166	654	611	468	330	716	277	208
5	593	254	745	287	936	466	868	515	930	391	891	594	302	228	554	906	881	433

- To generate random currency values between 100.00 and 999.99 with two decimal places in a 5-row by 9-column block:
  =RANDARRAY(5,9,10000,99999,TRUE)/100

A1		∨ ⋮ ✕ ✓ *fx* ∨	=RANDARRAY(5,9,10000,99999,TRUE)/100					
◢	A	B	C	D	E	F	G	H	I
1	584.8	531.99	597.96	414.32	511.05	473.02	253.94	492.73	978.46
2	118.93	837.04	228.36	983.08	323.37	900.49	697.58	325.82	647.6
3	645.88	422.67	815.91	640.45	911.54	265.89	603.78	896.74	254.9
4	543.11	893.66	676.14	191.89	824.45	804.36	817.96	213.35	473.59
5	930.65	818.97	966.25	649.16	260.98	320.91	486.87	570.81	524.39

Shift Your Rounding to the Left

The ROUND function is generally used to round numbers to the right of the decimal point. For example,

- =ROUND(A6, 2)
  rounds the value in cell A6 to 2 decimal places

- =ROUND(A6, 1)
  rounds the value in cell A6 to 1 decimal place

- =ROUND(A6, 0)
  rounds the value in cell A6 to the nearest whole number

However, by using a negative value as the second argument of the function, you can round numbers to the nearest 10, 100, 1000, etc. For example,

- =ROUND(A6, -1)
  rounds the value in cell A6 to the nearest 10

- =ROUND(A6, -2)
  rounds the value in cell A6 to the nearest 100

- =ROUND(A6, -3)
  rounds the value in cell A6 to the nearest 1000

Round to Any Multiple

The **MROUND** function rounds any number to a multiple that you specify.

The syntax of the function is;
=MROUND(number,multiple)
where;
Number is the value to round.
Multiple is the multiple to which you want to round the number.

Following are some examples of the MROUND function.

- Rounds the number in cell A1 to the nearest 10;
  =MROUND(A1,10)
  if the value in A1 was 32 the result would be 30

if the value in A1 was 35 the result would be 40
if the value in A1 was 38 the result would be 40

• Rounds the number in cell A1 to the nearest 100;
=MROUND(A1,100)
if the value in A1 was 29 the result would be 0
if the value in A1 was 167 the result would be 200

• Rounds the number in cell A1 to the nearest 0.05 (ie: five cents);
=MROUND(A1,0.05)
if the value in A1 was 9.02 the result would be 9.00
if the value in A1 was 9.03 the result would be 9.05
if the value in A1 was 9.07 the result would be 9.05
if the value in A1 was 9.08 the result would be 9.10

Ceiling and Floor Functions

Two useful rounding functions are **CEILING** and **FLOOR**. The CEILING function rounds away from zero to the nearest significance you designate. The FLOOR function always rounds toward zero to the nearest significance.

The syntax of the functions are;
=CEILING(number,significance)
=FLOOR(number,significance)
where;
Number is the value to round.
Significance is the multiple to which you want to round.

One use for these functions is in currency calculations, to always round up (with CEILING) or always round down (with FLOOR) to the desired currency fraction. The significance argument dictates the currency. Following are some examples of these functions.

• To the nearest 5 cents;
=CEILING(5.16,.05) results in 5.20
=FLOOR(5.16,.05) results in 5.15

• To the nearest 10 cents;
=CEILING(5.16,.1) results in 5.20
=FLOOR(5.16,.1) results in 5.10

• To the nearest 25 cents;
=CEILING(5.16,.25) results in 5.25
=FLOOR(5.16,.25) results in 5.00

Conditional Counting

The **COUNTIF** function counts the number of cells within a range that meet a given criteria.

The syntax of the function is;
=COUNTIF(range,criteria)
where;
Range is the range of cells from which you want to count.
Criteria is a number, expression, or text that defines the cells to be counted.

Following are some examples of the COUNTIF function.

- Counts the number of cells in the range called "data" that contain the value 12;
  =COUNTIF(DATA,12)

- Counts the number of cells in the range called "data" that contain the values
  1 or 12;
  =COUNTIF(DATA,1)+COUNTIF(DATA,12)

- Counts the number of cells in the range called "data" that contain a negative value;
  =COUNTIF(DATA,"<0")

- Counts the number of non-zero values in the range called "data";
  =COUNTIF(DATA,"<>0")

- Counts the number of cells in the range called "data" that contain a value between 1 and 10 (including 1 and 10);
  =COUNTIF(DATA,">=1")-COUNTIF(DATA,">=10")

- Counts the number of cells in the range called "data" that contain the word "yes" (not case sensitive);
  =COUNTIF(DATA,"YES")

- Counts the number of cells in the range called "data" that contain any text; =COUNTIF(DATA,"*")

- Counts the number of cells in the range called "data" containing three-letter words;
  =COUNTIF(DATA,"???")

Converting Units

The **CONVERT** function allows you to convert measurements from one system to another, eg: degrees Fahrenheit to degrees Celsius.

The syntax for the function is;
=CONVERT(number,from_unit,to_unit)
where;
Number is the value in from_units to convert.
From_unit is the code representing the measurement unit that you want to convert from.
To_unit is the code representing the measurement unit that you want to convert to.

For example, to convert the value in cell B1 from degrees Celsius to degrees Fahrenheit the following formula would be used.
=CONVERT(B1,"C","F")

To convert the value in cell B1 from inches to centimetres the following formula would be used.
=CONVERT(B1,"in","cm")

You can use the CONVERT function to perform conversions in the areas of weight, volume, distance, time, pressure, energy, force, power, magnetism, and a few others.

A complete list of measurement unit codes for the CONVERT function can be found in Excel's online help. Press **F1** to display the help panel and in the search box, type "convert function" and press **Enter**.

Note: The "from" and "to" codes used with this function are case sensitive, eg: a lowercase "c" is the code for calories and an uppercase "C" is the code for degrees Celsius.

Shortcuts for Entering the Current Date & Time

To quickly enter the current date into a cell, press **CTRL+;**

To quickly enter the current time into a cell, press **CTRL+SHIFT+;**
Both of these shortcuts simply enter the current date or time into the cell – the values do not automatically update.

To force Excel to automatically update the date and time values in a cell, a formula must be used. There are two functions that will achieve this;
=NOW()
and
=TODAY()

The =NOW() function returns both the date and the time, the =TODAY() function only returns the date value.

Note: The format of dates and times can be modified via the **Number** tab in the **Format Cells** dialog box.

Date Difference Function

The **DATEDIF** function calculates the time difference between two dates.

The syntax of the function is;
=DATEDIF (Date1, Date2, Interval)
where;
Date1 is the first date.
Date2 is the second date and must be greater than (ie: later) than Date1.
Interval indicates the unit of time that is used to calculate the result and can be either "d" (days), "m" (months) or "y" (years). The interval code must be entered in quotation marks when including it in the function, unless it is stored in a worksheet cell (in which case the code does not appear in quotation marks and the cell reference is used in the function).

In the spreadsheet shown below, the following DATEDIF functions are used.

•   In cell C2 the formula calculates the number of days between the dates in cells A2 and B2;
    =DATEDIF(A2,B2,"d")

- In cell D2 the formula calculates the number of months between the dates in cells A2 and B2;
  =DATEDIF(A2,B2,"m")

- In cell E2 the formula calculates the number of years between the dates in cells A2 and B2;
  =DATEDIF(A2,B2,"y")

E2		✓ : ╳ ✓ *fx* ✓	=DATEDIF(A2,B2,"y")		
◢	A	B	C	D	E
1	Start Date	End Date	Difference (Days)	Difference (Months)	Difference (Years)
2	5/06/1999	30/10/2016	6357	208	17
3	1/06/1974	16/10/1978	1598	52	4
4	7/06/2015	7/04/2019	1400	46	3
5	23/03/1979	9/08/2025	16941	556	46
6	11/06/2001	17/03/2003	644	21	1

Calculate Month Ends and Number of Days in a Month

The EOMONTH function returns the last day of a month, based on a starting date and the number of months before or after it.

The syntax of the function is;
=EOMONTH(start_date, months)
where;
start_date is the date you begin from.
months is the number of months forward (positive) or backward (negative) from the start date.

For example, if cell A1 contains 18/06/25
=EOMONTH(A1, 3)
returns 30/09/25 when formatted as a date (i.e. the last day of the month three months after June).

You can also use EOMONTH to find the number of days in a month, for example if cell A1 contains 18/06/25:
=DAY(EOMONTH(A1, 0))
returns 30, as June has 30 days. If cell A1 contained 18/7/25, the result of the formula would be 31, as July has 31 days.

This makes EOMONTH useful for working with due dates, maturity dates, or quickly checking how many days a given month has.

Calculate the Fraction of a Year Between Two Dates

The YEARFRAC function works out what portion of a year falls between two dates, based on the exact number of days.

In the following example:
=YEARFRAC(A2, B2)

C2	✓ : ✗ ✓ fx ✓ =YEARFRAC(A2, B2)		
	A	B	C
1	**Start Date**	**End Date**	**Fraction of a Year**
2	1/01/2025	27/08/2025	0.655555556
3	27/01/2025	23/03/2025	0.155555556

returns 0.65 – meaning the period between the start date in A2 and the end date in B2 is about 65% of a year (format the result as a percentage to display it this way).

This can be useful in financial models, project planning, or any situation where you need to measure time as part of a year.

Calculate the Number of Working Days Between Dates

The **NETWORKDAYS** function is used to calculate the number of working days between two dates.

The syntax of the function is;
=NETWORKDAYS(start_date, end_date, holidays)
where;
Start_date is a date that represents the start date.
End_date is a date that represents the end date.
Holidays is an optional list of one or more dates to exclude from the working calendar, such as public holidays or annual leave dates. The list can be a range

of cells (the range of holidays can be named to make it easier to include in the function).

In the example below, the NETWORKDAYS function is used to calculate the "Working Days to Complete" between the start and end dates of various projects. Weekend dates and dates defined as holidays (cells G2:H6) are not included in the calculation. The formula in cell D2 is;
=NETWORKDAYS(B2,C2,$G$2:$H$6)

D2			f_x	=NETWORKDAYS(B2,C2,$G$2:$H$6)				
	A	B	C	D	E	F	G	H
1		Start Date	Finish Date	Working Days to Complete			Holidays	
2	Project 1	1/01/2025	22/04/2025	76			1/01/2025	25/04/2025
3	Project 2	23/03/2025	8/04/2025	12			27/01/2025	9/06/2025
4	Project 3	5/06/2025	22/10/2025	98			18/04/2025	6/10/2025
5	Project 4	17/11/2025	19/12/2025	25			19/04/2025	25/12/2025
6							21/04/2025	26/12/2025

Calculating Workdays into the Future

The **WORKDAY** function is used to calculate the date that is a specified number of working days from a start date.
The syntax of the function is;
=WORKDAY(start_date,days,holidays)
where;
Start_date is a date that represents the start date.
Days is the number of working (non weekend / non holiday) days before or after the start_date. A positive value yields a future date, a negative value yields a past date.
Holidays is an optional list of one or more dates to exclude from the working calendar, such as public holidays or annual leave dates. The list can be a range of cells (the range of holidays can be named to make it easier to include in the function).

In the example below, the WORKDAY function is used to calculate the "Finish Date" of a number of projects, based on a starting date and the estimated number of working days it will take to complete the project.

Weekend dates and dates defined as holidays (cells G2:H6) are not included in the calculation. The formula in cell D2 is;
=WORKDAY(B2,C2,$G$2:$H$6)

| D2 | ⌄ | : | × | ✓ | f_x ⌄ | =WORKDAY(B2,C2,$G$2:$H$6) |

◢	A	B	C	D	E	F	G	H
1		Start Date	Working Days to Complete	Finish Date			Holidays	
2	Project 1	1/01/2025	76	22/04/2025			1/01/2025	25/04/2025
3	Project 2	12/03/2025	19	8/04/2025			27/01/2025	9/06/2025
4	Project 3	5/06/2025	21	7/07/2025			18/04/2025	6/10/2025
5	Project 4	17/11/2025	24	19/12/2025			19/04/2025	25/12/2025
6							21/04/2025	26/12/2025

Converting the Case of Text

Excel provides three functions that can be used to change the case of text in a cell. These functions are;

UPPER   Converts the text to uppercase.

LOWER   Converts the text to lowercase.

PROPER   Converts the first letter of each word to uppercase, remaining letters to lowercase.

The syntax of the functions are;
=UPPER(text)
=LOWER(text)
=PROPER(text)
where;
Text is a cell containing the text that you want to convert the case of.

These functions can be useful when text has been imported from another source and needs to be reformatted in Excel.

NAME	UPPER	LOWER	PROPER
hEATHER cLEARY	HEATHER CLEARY	heather cleary	Heather Cleary
mICHELLE gibbs	MICHELLE GIBBS	michelle gibbs	Michelle Gibbs
sAM tAMONE	SAM TAMONE	sam tamone	Sam Tamone
kENNETH Kwok	KENNETH KWOK	kenneth kwok	Kenneth Kwok
jILLIAN hOWELL	JILLIAN HOWELL	jillian howell	Jillian Howell
Anna MaRJANOVIC	ANNA MARJANOVIC	anna marjanovic	Anna Marjanovic

Joining Cells Together

The **TEXTJOIN** function is used to combine the contents of multiple cells into a single string. It is especially useful when data is imported from a text file or database and needs to be reformatted.

With TEXTJOIN, you specify a delimiter (such as a space, comma, or dash) that will be inserted between each value. You also choose whether to ignore empty cells. For example the formula:
=TEXTJOIN(" ", TRUE, A1:A4)
joins the contents of cells A1 through A4, placing a space between each value, and ignoring any blank cells.

In the example below, the first names and surnames of each employee are joined together by the formulas in Column C. The formula in cell C2 is:
=TEXTJOIN(" ", TRUE, A2, B2)

C2		fx	=TEXTJOIN(" ", TRUE, A2, B2)	
	A	B	C	D
	First Name	Surname	Full Name	
2	John	Sortwell	John Sortwell	
3	Sammy	Soumen	Sammy Soumen	
4	Phillip	Baxter	Phillip Baxter	
5	Grainne	Wolfe	Grainne Wolfe	
6	Blesy	Chalakkal	Blesy Chalakkal	
7	Esther	Bosman	Esther Bosman	

You can also use words or phrases as delimiters. For example, the formula:
=TEXTJOIN(" and ", TRUE, A1,B1)
joins the values of A1 and B1, placing the word "and" with spaces between them.

In the following example, a new accounting code is to be created. The formulas in column E join together the codes from columns A through to D.

The formula in cell E2 is;
=TEXTJOIN("", TRUE, A2:D2)

In this case, no delimiter is used, so the four values are joined directly together into one code.

| E2 | ⌄ ⋮ ✕ ✓ *fx* ⌄ | =TEXTJOIN("", TRUE, A2:D2) |

◢	A	B	C	D	E
1	Org Code	Process	Activity	Element Code	New Code
2	081	052	070	21000	08105207021000
3	081	052	070	21001	08105207021001
4	081	052	070	21200	08105207021200
5	081	059	075	26406	08105907526406
6	081	059	076	21001	08105907621001
7	081	059	076	21010	08105907621010
8	082	060	251	21013	08206025121013
9	082	060	098	21014	08206009821014
10	082	052	251	21200	08205225121200
11	082	052	251	26103	08205225126103
12	082	052	049	13010	08205204913010

Extracting Words from a Text String

Whilst the TEXTJOIN function can be used to join cells together (refer to "*Joining Cells Together*"), the **TEXTBEFORE and TEXTAFTER** function can be used to extract words from a text string. Take the following example of names, which includes middle names and initials.

◢	A
1	Ryan M. Nelson
2	Matthew Fulton
3	Christine Dehlsen
4	Ken D. Francis
5	Anne-Marie Holder
6	Benjamin Charles Edward Thomas

The TEXTBEFORE function returns the portion of text that appears before a specified character or string (the delimiter). The syntax of the function is;
=TEXTBEFORE(text, delimiter, instance_num, match_mode, match_end, if_not_found)
where;
text is the cell or text string you want to split.
delimiter is the character(s) to search for (e.g. " ", "-", ",").
instance_num is an optional argument specifying the occurrence of the delimiter to use, with the default of 1 (the first). Negative numbers work from the end (-1 is the last).
match_mode (optional) – 0 = case-sensitive (default), 1 = case-insensitive.
match_end (optional) – 0 = delimiter must be found before end of text (default),
1 = allow delimiter at end of text.
if_not_found is an optional argument specifying the value to return if the delimiter isn't found (instead of an error).

To extract each person's first name, enter the following formula in cell B1.
=TEXTBEFORE(A1, " ")

This formula can be copied down column B and should produce the following results.

B1	✓ ⋮ ✕ ✓ *fx* ✓	=TEXTBEFORE(A1, " ")	
	A	B	C
1	Ryan M. Nelson	Ryan	
2	Matthew Fulton	Matthew	
3	Christine Dehlsen	Christine	
4	Ken D. Francis	Ken	
5	Anne-Marie Holder	Anne-Marie	
6	Benjamin Charles Edward Thomas	Benjamin	

To extract each person's last name, enter the following formula in cell C1.
=TEXTAFTER(A1, " ", -1)

This formula can then be copied down column C and should produce the following results.

C1	✓ ⋮ ✕ ✓ *fx* ✓	=TEXTAFTER(A1, " ", -1)	
	A	B	C
1	Ryan M. Nelson	Ryan	Nelson
2	Matthew Fulton	Matthew	Fulton
3	Christine Dehlsen	Christine	Dehlsen
4	Ken D. Francis	Ken	Francis
5	Anne-Marie Holder	Anne-Marie	Holder
6	Benjamin Charles Edward Thomas	Benjamin	Thomas

Using the TRIM Function

The **TRIM** function removes excess spaces from text strings in a spreadsheet. This is a useful function for data that has been imported into Excel and contains several spaces between words. The TRIM function removes all excess spaces (it leaves one space between words).

In the following example the TRIM function is used to remove the excess spacing from text which has been imported into Excel. The formula in E2 is;
=TRIM(A2)

| E2 | ⌄ : ✕ ✓ *fx* ⌄ | =TRIM(A2) |

◢	A	B	C	D	E	F	G
1	**Imported Data**				**Trimmed Data**		
2	Charles	Franklin			Charles Franklin		
3	Benjamin	Charles	Edward	Thomas	Benjamin Charles Edward Thomas		
4	Sarah	J	Henderson		Sarah J Henderson		

Counting Unique Items

When working with large datasets, it's often useful to quickly see how many unique values are present across a range of cells. Excel makes this easy with dynamic array functions such as UNIQUE and TOCOL, which can filter out duplicates in a single step.

The following formula will count the number of unique entries in a range. Assuming the range of entries are in cells A13:T22:
=ROWS(UNIQUE(TOCOL(A1:T22,1)))

| D26 | ⌄ : ✕ ✓ *fx* ⌄ | =ROWS(UNIQUE(TOCOL(A1:T22,1))) |

◢	A	B	C	D	E	F	G	⊦
1	EL-947	CN-241	EL-544	ET-515	CN-735	EL-792	ET-448	EL-8:
2	EL-718	ET-414	EL-672	CN-698	ET-869	CN-722	EL-155	ET-9:
3	ET-925	EL-279	CN-171	ET-928	CN-844	ET-840	CN-353	ET-6:
4	CN-646	EL-825	CN-254	CN-316	EL-525	CN-364	ET-825	CN-4
5	EL-111	CN-338	ET-968	CN-355	ET-192	EL-685	ET-195	CN-5
6	ET-532	ET-325	EL-514	EL-863	EL-570	EL-207	EL-765	CN-5
7	EL-764	EL-218	CN-577	CN-230	ET-581	EL-901	ET-679	EL-5:
8	EL-586	ET-579	EL-730	CN-568	EL-969	ET-230	EL-520	EL-7:
9	EL-355	ET-376	ET-111	ET-840	ET-457	ET-939	ET-281	ET-3:
10	ET-673	ET-182	CN-507	ET-400	ET-413	CN-199	EL-880	CN-9
11	ET-974	ET-411	ET-264	EL-560	CN-328	ET-515	CN-939	EL-5:
12	EL-426	ET-450	CN-851	EL-881	CN-863	ET-268	CN-346	CN-8
13	EL-660	CN-809	CN-323	EL-484	CN-594	EL-839	CN-486	ET-4:
14	CN-349	EL-725	CN-392	CN-429	CN-402	ET-851	ET-826	ET-3:
15	ET-728	ET-852	ET-480	CN-140	EL-566	CN-756	ET-966	ET-7:
16	EL-367	EL-811	EL-298	ET-189	CN-124	EL-598	ET-948	ET-6:
17	CN-799	EL-141	EL-303	EL-232	EL-782	CN-963	CN-382	EL-7:
18	EL-745	EL-530	CN-931	ET-595	CN-498	EL-318	EL-949	ET-1:
19	CN-952	EL-556	ET-814	EL-265	CN-869	EL-166	CN-679	EL-3:
20	CN-600	CN-514	EL-681	ET-139	ET-715	CN-558	EL-164	CN-1
21	CN-294	ET-913	ET-169	EL-553	ET-876	ET-926	CN-327	ET-1:
22	CN-155	ET-701	ET-220	ET-700	EL-932	CN-956	EL-208	ET-1:
23								
24		**Number of Items**			440			
25								
26		**Number of Unique Items**			409			

Find the Most Common Value(s) in a Range

There are two functions that find the most common value in a range:
MODE.SNGL returns a single most frequently occurring number in a range.
MODE.MULT returns all the values that occur with the same highest frequency.

For example, in the following worksheet, the formula:

=MODE.SNGL(A1:A7)
returns the value of 4 (the first number that occurs most frequently)
and

=MODE.MULT(A1:A7)
returns the values of 4 and 6 (as they are both the most frequently occurring values)

	A	B
1	2	
2	4	
3	4	
4	6	
5	6	
6	8	
7	10	
8		
9	MODE.SNGL	4
10		
11	MODE.MULT	4
12		6

Using the LARGE and SMALL Functions

The **LARGE** and **SMALL** functions work in a similar way to the MAX (maximum) and MIN (minimum) functions, except that they find the "nth" largest or smallest value in a range.

Following are some examples of the LARGE and SMALL functions.

- Returns the fifth largest number in cells A1 to C15;
  =LARGE(A1:C15,5)

- Returns the ninth smallest number in cells A1 to C15;
  =SMALL(A1:C15,9)

If you combine the AVERAGE function and either the LARGE or SMALL function you can create a formula that averages the top or bottom values from a range. For example, the following formula averages the top 5 values from the range A1 to C15;

=AVERAGE(LARGE(A1:C15,{1,2,3,4,5}))

Return the Label for the Maximum Value

Often you'll have two related columns – one with labels (such as dates, names, or categories) and another with numbers (such as sales, scores, or totals). If you want to know which label corresponds to the highest number, you can combine lookup functions to return the value from one column that matches the maximum in another.

For example, if you have station locations in Column A and passenger numbers in Column B, the following formula will return the station name with the highest number of passengers:
=INDEX(A2:A20, MATCH(MAX(B2:B20), B2:B20, 0))

| B22 | ∨ : ✕ ✓ fx ∨ | =INDEX(A2:A20, MATCH(MAX(B2:B20), B2:B20, 0)) |

⊿	A	B	C	D	E	F	G	H
1	Station	Estimated Weekly Passengers						
2	Lidcombe	141,071						
3	Auburn	161,008						
4	Clyde	11,032						
5	Granville	79,016						
6	Harris Park	29,617						
7	Parramatta	412,972						
8	Westmead	64,190						
9	Wentworthville	13,440						
10	Pendle Hill	29,064						
11	Toongabbie	27,195						
12	Seven Hills	56,770						
13	Blacktown	167,237						
14	Doonside	25,977						
15	Rooty Hill	32,921						
16	Mount Druitt	64,246						
17	St Marys	41,720						
18	Werrington	10,521						
19	Kingswood	20,370						
20	Penrith	72,478						
21								
22	*Highest Passenger Numbers*	*Parramatta*						

Using the RANK Function

The **RANK.EQ** function is used to display the positional order that a number holds within a list of values.

The syntax of the function is;
=RANK.EQ(number,ref)
where;
Number is the number that you want to find the ranking of.
Ref is the range of cells containing all the values that are being ranked. The range used in the "ref" argument should be made absolute so that doesn't change when you copy the formula.

In the following example the function is used to rank a group of student exam scores. Cell C2 contains the following formula;
=RANK.EQ(B2,$B$2:$B$16)

C2			✓ : ✗ ✓ *fx* ✓	=RANK.EQ(B2,$B$2:$B$16)		
	A	B	C	D	E	F
1	Student	Mark	Rank			
2	Aarav	72	7			
3	Angela	85	5			
4	Chantell	89	3			
5	Clare	89	3			
6	Heather	60	14			
7	James	91	2			
8	Mei Ling	61	13			
9	Meredith	65	10			
10	Omar	69	8			
11	Patrick	81	6			
12	Paul	62	12			
13	Priya	66	9			
14	Ryuichi	92	1			
15	Scott	47	15			
16	Trevor	63	11			

Note: Where more than one item has the same value (in this example Chantell and Clare have the same mark), all values are given the same rank and the next ranking sequence(s) are skipped (in this example no student has rank number 4).

Filter Data with a Formula

The **FILTER** function lets you extract a subset of data from a range based on one or more conditions, with the results "spilling" automatically into the surrounding cells.

The syntax of the function is;
=FILTER(array, include, [if_empty])
where;
array (required) is the range or array you want to filter (e.g. a table or list).
include (required) is the condition(s) that determine which rows/columns to keep. This must return a TRUE/FALSE array of the same size as the rows or columns in array.
if_empty (optional) is what to return if no results match.

In the following example, the formula below is entered in cell I2 and displays the items that have a status of "Completed". If there are no orders with the status of "completed", a message stating "No completed orders" is displayed.

=FILTER(A2:F23, F2:F23="Completed", "No completed orders")

OrderID	Part	Category	Quantity	Total Value	Status
FAC3000	Gear	Mechanical	482	$407.52	In Progress
FAC3001	Pump	Hydraulic	9	$1,176.32	In Progress
FAC3002	Pump	Hydraulic	3	$2,734.72	Completed
FAC3003	Bearing	Mechanical	324	$847.01	Pending
FAC3004	Gear	Mechanical	458	$2,547.23	Pending
FAC3005	Bolt	Fasteners	286	$1,180.95	Pending
FAC3006	Nut	Fasteners	478	$2,263.87	Completed
FAC3007	Valve	Hydraulic	109	$2,038.79	Pending
FAC3008	Shaft	Mechanical	25	$2,016.28	Pending
FAC3009	Spring	Mechanical	488	$631.05	Backordered
FAC3010	Coupling	Mechanical	224	$755.00	Completed
FAC3011	Screw	Fasteners	485	$555.40	Completed
FAC3012	O-Ring	Sealing	462	$1,550.17	Backordered
FAC3013	Gear	Mechanical	50	$3,159.96	In Progress
FAC3014	Bolt	Fasteners	204	$2,062.31	Backordered
FAC3015	Pump	Hydraulic	7	$2,598.45	Completed
FAC3016	Bearing	Mechanical	460	$2,577.48	Backordered
FAC3017	Screw	Fasteners	481	$2,995.01	Pending
FAC3018	Screw	Fasteners	60	$1,582.29	Pending
FAC3019	Gasket	Sealing	358	$326.15	Backordered
FAC3020	Gear	Mechanical	114	$938.27	Completed
FAC3021	Bearing	Mechanical	245	$2,146.25	In Progress

Result:

OrderID	Part	Category	Quantity	Total Value	Status
FAC3002	Pump	Hydraulic	3	$2,734.72	Completed
FAC3006	Nut	Fasteners	478	$2,263.87	Completed
FAC3010	Coupling	Mechanical	224	$755.00	Completed
FAC3011	Screw	Fasteners	465	$555.40	Completed
FAC3015	Pump	Hydraulic	7	$2,598.45	Completed
FAC3020	Gear	Mechanical	114	$938.27	Completed

To specify multiple conditions, using the AND operator, multiply the different conditions in the formula. For example the following formula filters for products in the "Fasteners" category that have a status of "Pending".
=FILTER(A2:F23,(C2:C23="Fasteners")*(F2:F23="Pending"),"No matches")

OrderID	Part	Category	Quantity	Total Value	Status
FAC3000	Gear	Mechanical	482	$407.52	In Progress
FAC3001	Pump	Hydraulic	9	$1,176.32	In Progress
FAC3002	Pump	Hydraulic	3	$2,734.72	Completed
FAC3003	Bearing	Mechanical	324	$847.01	Pending
FAC3004	Gear	Mechanical	458	$2,547.23	Pending
FAC3005	Bolt	Fasteners	286	$1,180.95	Pending
FAC3006	Nut	Fasteners	478	$2,263.87	Completed
FAC3007	Valve	Hydraulic	109	$2,038.79	Pending
FAC3008	Shaft	Mechanical	25	$2,016.28	Pending
FAC3009	Spring	Mechanical	488	$631.05	Backordered
FAC3010	Coupling	Mechanical	224	$755.00	Completed
FAC3011	Screw	Fasteners	485	$555.40	Completed
FAC3012	O-Ring	Sealing	462	$1,550.17	Backordered
FAC3013	Gear	Mechanical	50	$3,159.96	In Progress
FAC3014	Bolt	Fasteners	204	$2,062.31	Backordered
FAC3015	Pump	Hydraulic	7	$2,598.45	Completed
FAC3016	Bearing	Mechanical	460	$2,577.48	Backordered
FAC3017	Screw	Fasteners	481	$2,995.01	Pending
FAC3018	Screw	Fasteners	60	$1,582.29	Pending
FAC3019	Gasket	Sealing	358	$326.15	Backordered
FAC3020	Gear	Mechanical	114	$938.27	Completed
FAC3021	Bearing	Mechanical	245	$2,146.25	In Progress

Result:

OrderID	Part	Category	Quantity	Total Value	Status
FAC3005	Bolt	Fasteners	286	$1,180.95	Pending
FAC3017	Screw	Fasteners	481	$2,995.01	Pending
FAC3018	Screw	Fasteners	60	$1,582.29	Pending

To find values within a range, use the AND operator along with the greater than, less than and equals signs as you would in other formulas and functions. For example, the following formula filters for total values over $2500.
=FILTER(A2:F23, E2:E23>2500, "No matches")

`=FILTER(A2:F23, E2:E23>2500, "No matches")`

OrderID	Part	Category	Quantity	Total Value	Status			OrderID	Part	Category	Quantity	Total Value	Status
FAC3000	Gear	Mechanical	482	$407.52	In Progress			FAC3002	Pump	Hydraulic	3	$2,734.72	Completed
FAC3001	Pump	Hydraulic	9	$1,176.32	In Progress			FAC3004	Gear	Mechanical	458	$2,547.23	Pending
FAC3002	Pump	Hydraulic	3	$2,734.72	Completed			FAC3013	Gear	Mechanical	50	$3,159.96	In Progress
FAC3003	Bearing	Mechanical	324	$847.01	Pending			FAC3015	Pump	Hydraulic	7	$2,598.45	Completed
FAC3004	Gear	Mechanical	458	$2,547.23	Pending			FAC3016	Bearing	Mechanical	460	$2,577.48	Backordered
FAC3005	Bolt	Fasteners	286	$1,180.95	Pending			FAC3017	Screw	Fasteners	481	$2,995.01	Pending
FAC3006	Nut	Fasteners	478	$2,263.87	Completed								
FAC3007	Valve	Hydraulic	109	$2,038.79	Pending								
FAC3008	Shaft	Mechanical	25	$2,016.28	Pending								
FAC3009	Spring	Mechanical	486	$631.05	Backordered								
FAC3010	Coupling	Mechanical	724	$755.00	Completed								
FAC3011	Screw	Fasteners	465	$555.40	Completed								
FAC3012	O-Ring	Sealing	462	$1,550.17	Backordered								
FAC3013	Gear	Mechanical	50	$3,159.96	In Progress								
FAC3014	Bolt	Fasteners	204	$2,062.31	Backordered								
FAC3015	Pump	Hydraulic	7	$2,598.45	Completed								
FAC3016	Bearing	Mechanical	460	$2,577.48	Backordered								
FAC3017	Screw	Fasteners	481	$2,995.01	Pending								
FAC3018	Screw	Fasteners	60	$1,582.29	Pending								
FAC3019	Gasket	Sealing	358	$326.15	Backordered								
FAC3020	Gear	Mechanical	114	$938.27	Completed								
FAC3021	Bearing	Mechanical	245	$2,146.25	In Progress								

To specify multiple conditions, using the OR operator, add the different conditions in the formula with the "+" sign. For example the following formula filters for parts that are either "Nut" or "Bolt" or "Valve".
**=FILTER(A2:F23,(B2:B23="Nut")+(B2:B23="Bolt")+(B2:B23="Valve")
,"No matches")**

`=FILTER(A2:F23,(B2:B23="Nut")+(B2:B23="Bolt")+(B2:B23="Valve"),"No matches")`

OrderID	Part	Category	Quantity	Total Value	Status			OrderID	Part	Category	Quantity	Total Value	Status
FAC3000	Gear	Mechanical	482	$407.52	In Progress			FAC3005	Bolt	Fasteners	286	$1,180.95	Pending
FAC3001	Pump	Hydraulic	9	$1,176.32	In Progress			FAC3006	Nut	Fasteners	478	$2,263.87	Completed
FAC3002	Pump	Hydraulic	3	$2,734.72	Completed			FAC3007	Valve	Hydraulic	109	$2,038.79	Pending
FAC3003	Bearing	Mechanical	324	$847.01	Pending			FAC3014	Bolt	Fasteners	204	$2,062.31	Backordered
FAC3004	Gear	Mechanical	458	$2,547.23	Pending								
FAC3005	Bolt	Fasteners	286	$1,180.95	Pending								
FAC3006	Nut	Fasteners	478	$2,263.87	Completed								
FAC3007	Valve	Hydraulic	109	$2,038.79	Pending								
FAC3008	Shaft	Mechanical	25	$2,016.28	Pending								
FAC3009	Spring	Mechanical	486	$631.05	Backordered								
FAC3010	Coupling	Mechanical	224	$755.00	Completed								
FAC3011	Screw	Fasteners	465	$555.40	Completed								
FAC3012	O-Ring	Sealing	462	$1,550.17	Backordered								
FAC3013	Gear	Mechanical	50	$3,159.96	In Progress								
FAC3014	Bolt	Fasteners	204	$2,062.31	Backordered								
FAC3015	Pump	Hydraulic	7	$2,598.45	Completed								
FAC3016	Bearing	Mechanical	460	$2,577.48	Backordered								
FAC3017	Screw	Fasteners	481	$2,995.01	Pending								
FAC3018	Screw	Fasteners	60	$1,582.29	Pending								
FAC3019	Gasket	Sealing	358	$326.15	Backordered								
FAC3020	Gear	Mechanical	114	$938.27	Completed								
FAC3021	Bearing	Mechanical	245	$2,146.25	In Progress								

WORKING
WITH
DATA

Be Careful of Hidden Rows When Sorting

When you sort a range that contains hidden rows, only the visible rows are sorted. The hidden rows remain in their original positions. As a result, when you unhide those rows, the records may appear out of order compared to the sorted data.

If you want the hidden rows to be sorted as well, you must unhide them before sorting. Alternatively, use filtering instead of manually hiding rows – filtered rows are automatically included in the sort when you clear the filter.

Reversing a Sort Operation

If you sort data and later want to restore the original order, you could use the **Undo** feature. This works well if you realise your mistake immediately, but it won't help if you decide to "unsort" the data much later (for example, after performing several other actions or saving and closing the file).

The following method lets you keep track of the original order of items in a list so you can restore it at any time:

1) Insert a new column to the list (preferably as the first column) and give it a heading such as "Original Order".

2) In this column, number each row (1, 2, 3, etc.) to represent the item's original position in the list. You can quickly create this sequence using AutoFill (see *Using the Fill Handle*).

3) Hide the column so it doesn't interfere with your view of the data.

4) If you need to restore the original order, unhide the column and sort it in ascending order.

Sorting in a Custom Order

Excel provides a facility to sort alphabetically or numerically in both ascending and descending order. However in some cases the order that you want to sort by may not be alphabetic or numeric at all. You can sort list items in a custom order by specifying the order of items in a custom list and then using this list as the basis for sorting.

In the following example, we want to sort the employees by "Department", in the following order — MANAGEMENT, ADMINISTRATION, and PRODUCTION.

	A	B	C	D
	Employee Code	First Name	Surname	Department
1				
2	D1510	Penelope	Ayre	PRODUCTION
3	A5235	Lyn	Daniels	ADMINISTRATION
4	C7544	Travis	Edwards	MANAGEMENT
5	C7209	David	Garvey	MANAGEMENT
6	B9615	Tim	Mielnik	PRODUCTION
7	C4875	Ryan	Nelson	ADMINISTRATION
8	A6508	Robyn	Ohlsen	ADMINISTRATION
9	B7335	Frank	Small	ADMINISTRATION
10	D2622	Alexander	Trethewy	ADMINISTRATION
11	D3872	Ingrid	Wheeler	MANAGEMENT

1) Create a custom list (refer to "*Creating a Custom AutoFill Series*") with the entries in the order that you want the data sorted.

2) Click anywhere in the column you want to sort (in this example, column D) and from the **Data** tab on the Ribbon, click on the **Sort** button. The "Sort" dialog box will be displayed.

3) In the **Sort by** drop-down list, select the field you want to sort by (in this example, Department)

4) From the drop-down list under the **Order** field, select **Custom List**.

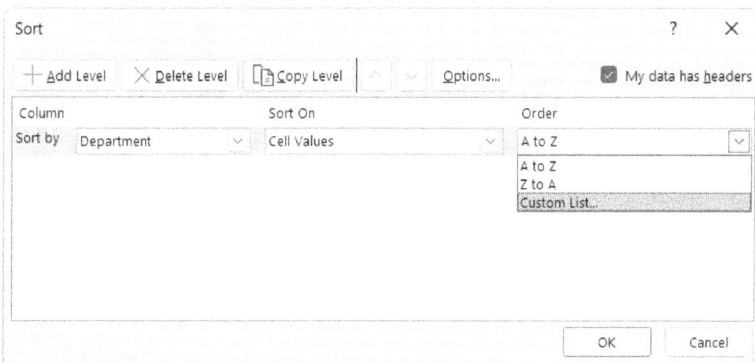

Sort			? ✕
+ Add Level ✕ Delete Level 📋 Copy Level ∧ ∨ Options...			☑ My data has headers
Column	Sort On	Order	
Sort by Department ∨	Cell Values ∨	A to Z ∨	
		A to Z	
		Z to A	
		Custom List...	
		OK Cancel	

5) Select the custom list representing the sort order that you want to use.

6) Click **OK** twice to complete the sort.

The data will be sorted in the order specified in the custom list.

	A	B	C	D
1	Employee Code	First Name	Surname	Department
2	C7544	Travis	Edwards	MANAGEMENT
3	C7209	David	Garvey	MANAGEMENT
4	D3872	Ingrid	Wheeler	MANAGEMENT
5	A5235	Lyn	Daniels	ADMINISTRATION
6	C4875	Ryan	Nelson	ADMINISTRATION
7	A6508	Robyn	Ohlsen	ADMINISTRATION
8	B7335	Frank	Small	ADMINISTRATION
9	D2622	Alexander	Trethewy	ADMINISTRATION
10	D1510	Penelope	Ayre	PRODUCTION
11	B9615	Tim	Mielnik	PRODUCTION

Filtering Entries from a List

Excel has an easy-to-use filtering tool called AutoFilter. When you activate the AutoFilter command, a drop-down arrow appears in the heading of each column, allowing you to filter the records in your list. The drop-down list includes all the unique values from that column, as well as some additional filtering options.

1) Place the cell pointer anywhere within your list.

2) Select the **Data** tab on the Ribbon.

3) In the **Sort & Filter** group, click the **Filter** button.

Once activated, you can click the drop-down arrow for any column heading and choose the values you want to display in your filtered view. The example below shows the list of values available for the "Flavour" field.

	A	B	C	D	E
1	Year ▾	Flavour ▾	Region ▾	Units Sol ▾	Sales ▾

A↓ Sort A to Z

Z↓ Sort Z to A

Sort by Color   >

Sheet View   >

▽ Clear Filter From "Flavour"

Filter by Color   >

Text Filters   >

[Search]

☑ (Select All)
☑ Butter Pecan
☑ Chocolate
☑ Coffee
☑ Pistachio
☑ Strawberry
☑ Vanilla
☑ Vanilla Fudge

[OK] [Cancel]

			Units Sold	Sales
			29000	$87,000
			38000	$114,000
			33000	$99,000
			45000	$135,000
			114000	$342,000
			129000	$387,000
			88000	$264,000
			146000	$438,000
			164000	$492,000
			177000	$531,000
			148000	$444,000
			191000	$573,000
			49000	$147,000
			54000	$162,000
			62000	$186,000
			71000	$213,000
			85000	$255,000
			76000	$228,000
			91000	$273,000
			102000	$306,000
			139000	$417,000
			123000	$369,000
			117000	$351,000
			145000	$435,000
			151000	$453,000
			146000	$438,000
28	2024	Vanilla Fudge	South	122000	$366,000
29	2024	Vanilla Fudge	West	160000	$480,000

Once data from the list has been filtered, the drop-down arrow in the filtered column changes to a funnel icon. The row numbers in the list area also appear in blue, indicating that a filter is active.

If you apply a filter to more than one column, the filters work together (in database terminology this is known as an "AND" operator). For example, if you selected "Vanilla" as the Flavour and "East" as the Region, the list would display all the sales of Vanilla in the East region.

To remove filtering from a column, click the drop-down list for that column and select **Clear Filter From [Column Name]** or enable the **(Select All)** option.

A↓ Sort A to Z

Z↓ Sort Z to A

Sort by Color   >

Sheet View

🔽 Clear Filter From "Flavour"   To remove a filter from a
                                        column, click the "Clear
Filter by Color   >   Filter From..." option

Text Filters   >

Search

☑ ■ (Select All)   or
   ☐ Butter Pecan
   ☐ Chocolate   enable the "(Select All)
   ☐ Coffee   option
   ☐ Pistachio
   ☐ Strawberry
   ☑ Vanilla
   ☑ Vanilla Fudge

[OK] [Cancel]

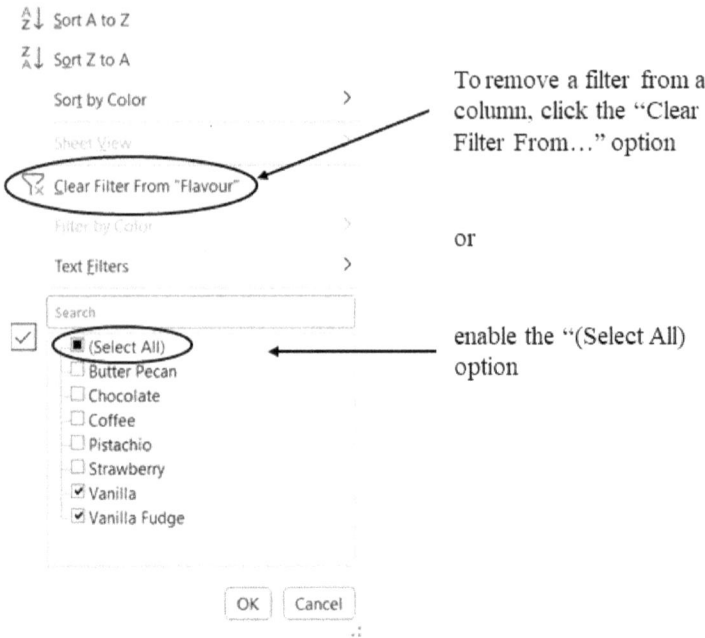

To remove all filtering (and the drop-down arrows from the columns), go to the **Data** tab on the Ribbon and de-select the **Filter** button.

Filtering Data with Slicers

Slicers provide an interactive way to filter data in Excel. They give you clickable buttons to filter your data quickly, and they clearly show which filters are applied. This is especially useful when working with large lists, such as customer records, sales transactions, or employee rosters.

1)   Click anywhere inside the range of data to filter and press **CTRL+T**. The "Create Table" dialog box will be displayed.

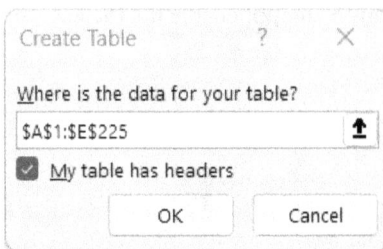

Create Table   ?   ✕

Where is the data for your table?

$A$1:$E$225   ⬆

☑ My table has headers

          [OK]   [Cancel]

2) Click **OK** to confirm the data range for the table.

3) Select the **Table Design** tab on the Ribbon and from the **Tools** group, click **Insert Slicer** button. The "Insert Slicers" dialog box will be displayed, showing the column headers from the data table.

Insert Slicers   ?   ✕

☐ Year
☐ Flavour
☐ Region
☐ Units Sold
☐ Sales

OK   Cancel

4) Enable the column(s) you want to filter by and click **OK**. A slicer box will appear on your worksheet for each field that you have selected, displaying all of the entries for that field. The slicer boxes can be positioned wherever you like on the screen.

Year	Flavour	Region	Units Sold	Sales
2023	Butter Pecan	East	29,000	$87,000
2023	Butter Pecan	North	38,000	$114,000
2023	Butter Pecan	South	33,000	$99,000
2023	Butter Pecan	West	45,000	$135,000
2023	Chocolate	East	114,000	$342,000
2023	Chocolate	North	129,000	$387,000
2023	Chocolate	South	88,000	$264,000
2023	Chocolate	West	146,000	$438,000
2023	Coffee	East	164,000	$492,000
2023	Coffee	North	177,000	$531,000
2023	Coffee	South	148,000	$444,000
2023	Coffee	West	191,000	$573,000
2023	Pistachio	East	49,000	$147,000
2023	Pistachio	North	54,000	$162,000
2023	Pistachio	South	62,000	$186,000
2023	Pistachio	West	71,000	$213,000
2023	Strawberry	East	85,000	$255,000
2023	Strawberry	North	76,000	$228,000
2023	Strawberry	South	91,000	$273,000
2023	Strawberry	West	102,000	$306,000
2023	Vanilla	East	139,000	$417,000
2023	Vanilla	North	123,000	$369,000
2023	Vanilla	South	117,000	$351,000
2023	Vanilla	West	145,000	$435,000
2023	Vanilla Fudge	East	151,000	$453,000
2023	Vanilla Fudge	North	146,000	$438,000
2023	Vanilla Fudge	South	122,000	$366,000

Year
2023
2024
2025

Region
East
North
South
West

Flavour
Butter Pecan
Chocolate
Coffee
Pistachio
Strawberry
Vanilla
Vanilla Fudge

5) Use the individual buttons from each slicer box to filter the table.

6) To select multiple buttons from the slicer box, click the **Multi-Select** ⅍≣ button in the top right of the slicer box.

7) To clear the filter, click the ▽× **Clear Filter** button in the top right of the slicer box.

8) To remove the slicer box, click on it once and press **Delete** on the keyboard.

Slicers are especially useful with PivotTables and PivotCharts, as they let you filter by categories like region, product, or team with a single click.

Filtering Values

When working with AutoFilters (refer to "*Filtering Entries from a List*"), columns containing values allow you to use a series of special numeric filters (e.g. greater than, less than, between, top 10, above average, below average).

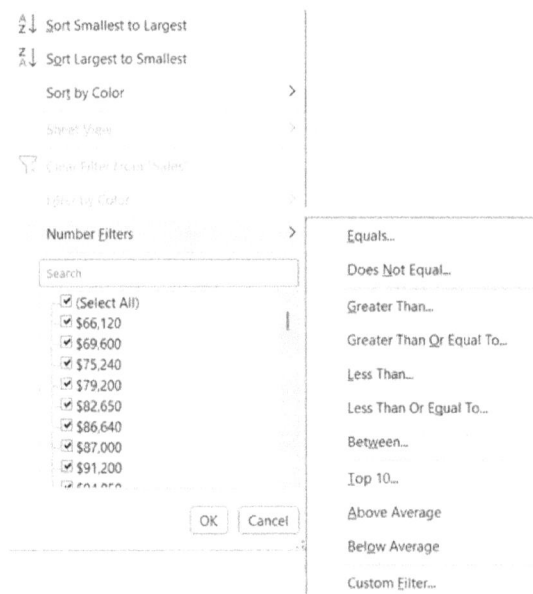

The following diagram shows the records with a sales value between 300,000 and 350,000.

	A	B	C	D	E	F	G	H	I	J	K	L	M
1	Year	Flavour	Region	Units Sol	Sales								
6	2024	Chocolate	East	114000	$342,000	Custom Autofilter						?	X
21	2024	Strawberry	West	102000	$306,000	Show rows where:							
36	2024	Chocolate	South	114400	$343,200	Sales							
46	2024	Strawberry	East	110500	$331,500								
63	2024	Chocolate	North	103200	$309,600	is greater than or equa... ∨	300000						∨
78	2024	Vanilla	East	111200	$333,600	● And ○ Or							
81	2024	Vanilla	West	116000	$348,000	is less than or equal to ∨	350000						∨
101	2024	Pistachio	West	113600	$340,800								
118	2025	Chocolate	East	108300	$324,900	Use ? to represent any single character							
136	2025	Vanilla	South	111150	$333,450	Use * to represent any series of characters							
140	2025	Vanilla Fudge	South	115900	$347,700								
148	2025	Chocolate	South	108680	$326,040						OK		Cancel
158	2025	Strawberry	East	104975	$314,925								
160	2025	Strawberry	South	112385	$337,155								
177	2025	Chocolate	West	110960	$332,880								
180	2025	Coffee	South	112480	$337,440								
190	2025	Vanilla	East	105640	$316,920								
193	2025	Vanilla	West	110200	$330,600								
194	2025	Vanilla Fudge	East	114760	$344,280								
195	2025	Vanilla Fudge	North	110960	$332,880								
213	2025	Pistachio	West	107920	$323,760								
215	2025	Strawberry	North	115520	$346,560								

You could continue to filter by other columns, remembering that they act as additional AND filters, e.g. adding a filter for Chocolate flavour and East region would display records where the sales value was between 300,000 and 350,000, the flavour sold was Chocolate, and the sales region was East (in this example there would be 2 records).

The Top Ten AutoFilter

When working with numeric data in an AutoFilter (refer to "*Filtering Values*"), the **(Top 10…)** option can be used to filter the data. Selecting this option from the drop-down list on a numeric field allows you to perform the following actions.

1) Specify either the **Top** or **Bottom** records.

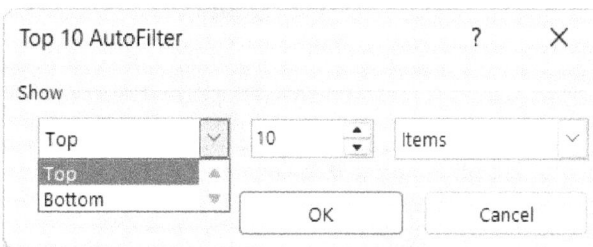

Top 10 AutoFilter   ?   X

Show

| Top ∨ | 10 | Items ∨ |
| Top |
| Bottom |

OK   Cancel

2) Change the number of records to retrieve.

Top 10 AutoFilter	?	✕
Show		
Top ⌄	20 ⏶⏷	Items ⌄
	OK	Cancel

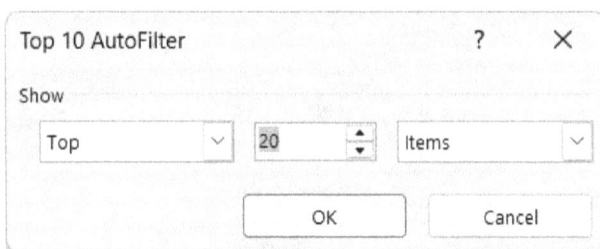

3) Specify whether you want to retrieve the number of **Items**, or the top/bottom **Percent** of items.

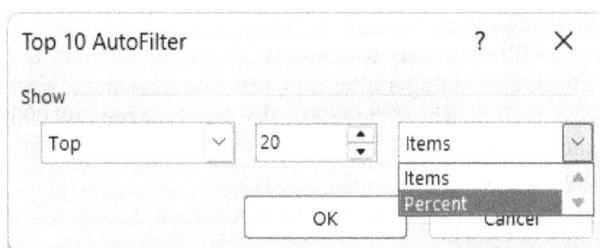

Top 10 AutoFilter	?	✕
Show		
Top ⌄	20 ⏶⏷	Items ⌄
		Items ⏶
	OK	Percent ⏷ Cancel

Calculating Values in a Filtered List

When you use the AutoFilter command (refer to "*Filtering Entries from a List*"), only the rows of data that meet the condition(s) you set are displayed – all other rows are temporarily hidden.

If you use the SUM function on a filtered list, Excel will still total all the values in the range, including those in hidden rows. This is often not what you want – for example, you might only want the total for the filtered (visible) items.

In this situation, the SUBTOTAL function is more useful because it calculates only the values in visible cells, ignoring those in hidden rows.

The syntax of the function is;
=SUBTOTAL(function_num,range)
where;
Function_num is a number (1 to 11) that specifies which function to use in calculating subtotals from the list. For example, the value "9" tells Excel to return the sum of the values. Other functions available are average (1), count (2), maximum (4), minimum (5), etc. Excel's online help feature contains a complete list of the function numbers and the calculations they represent.

Range is the range of cell references to be used in calculating the subtotal (not including headings).

In the following example, the database area is the range A1 to C16 and the objective is to total the "Sales" column based on different criteria that are specified using the AutoFilter feature.

If the SUM function was used, ie: =SUM(C2:C16), the total sales amount would be shown, regardless of the cells that were being displayed as a result of the AutoFilter.

However, the SUBTOTAL function will only sum the cells that are visible, hence the formula used in cell F1 is;
=SUBTOTAL(9,C2:C16)

The following diagram shows the result of the formula when all the data is showing.

	A	B	C	D	E	F
1	SalesPerso ▾	Item ▾	Sales ▾		TOTAL:	$30,071
2	Clifford	Furniture	$2,786			
3	Whitehead	Furniture	$2,627			
4	Clifford	Electrical	$1,448			
5	Clifford	Electrical	$886			
6	Tunstell	Furniture	$1,183			
7	Whitehead	Furniture	$542			
8	Whitehead	Furniture	$2,366			
9	Tunstell	Furniture	$2,137			
10	Whitehead	Electrical	$1,824			
11	Clifford	Electrical	$2,683			
12	Whitehead	Furniture	$2,180			
13	Tunstell	Electrical	$2,549			
14	Tunstell	Electrical	$3,126			
15	Whitehead	Electrical	$3,245			
16	Tunstell	Furniture	$489			

The next diagram shows the result of the formula when the list has been filtered to show only "Furniture" sold by "Whitehead".

⊿	A	B	C	D	E	F
1	**SalesPerso** ▼	**Item** ▼	**Sales** ▼		**TOTAL:**	**$7,715**
3	Whitehead	Furniture	$2,627			
7	Whitehead	Furniture	$542			
8	Whitehead	Furniture	$2,366			
12	Whitehead	Furniture	$2,180			

Note: Ensure that the formula appears in a cell that is not part of the list area (ie: use an area at the top or the bottom of the list area), otherwise the cell containing the formula may be hidden when particular criteria are selected from the AutoFilter.

Split Imported Data into Separate Columns

If you have information combined in a single column, such as data imported from other software or systems, the fields for each row (like names, addresses, or codes) often end up merged into one cell. Excel's Text to Columns tool makes it simple to split that data into separate, organised columns. With a few clicks, you can separate data by a consistent delimiter (such as a space or comma) and quickly organise it into clean, structured columns.

1) Select the cells you want to split.

2) Go to the **Data** tab on the Ribbon and from the **Data Tools** group, select **Text to Columns**. The "Convert Text to Columns Wizard" dialog box is displayed.

Convert Text to Columns Wizard - Step 1 of 3   ?   X

The Text Wizard has determined that your data is Delimited.

If this is correct, choose Next, or choose the data type that best describes your data.

Original data type

Choose the file type that best describes your data:

- ⦿ Delimited   - Characters such as commas or tabs separate each field.
- ◯ Fixed width   - Fields are aligned in columns with spaces between each field.

Preview of selected data:

```
1 Contact Name,Company,Address,Suburb,State,Postcode,Phone Number
2 Liam Turner,Orion Consulting,12 King St,Sydney,NSW,2000,(02) 9123 4567
3 Sophie Mitchell,BlueWave Tech,85 George St,Parramatta,NSW,2150,(02) 8899 1122
4 Ethan Clarke,Harbour Finance,44 Pacific Hwy,North Sydney,NSW,2060,(02) 8456 7890
5 Ava Johnson,UrbanWorks Design,22 Hunter St,Newcastle,NSW,2300,(02) 4978 6655
6 Noah Edwards,NextGen Retail,9 Church St,Hornsby,NSW,2077,(02) 9482 3000
```

Cancel   < Back   Next >   Finish

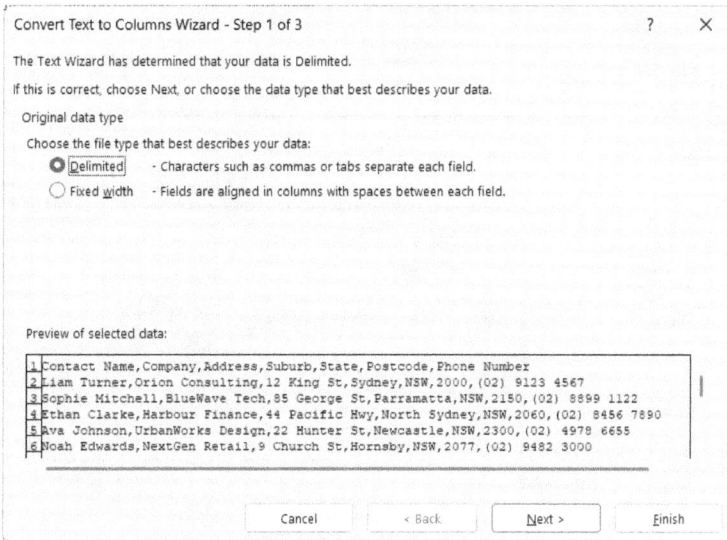

3) Select **Delimited** (for data separated by spaces, commas, etc.) or **Fixed Width** (if each field has a set number of characters).

4) Click **Next**, then if required specify the delimiter that separates each of the fields in your data.

5) Click **Finish**. Excel places the split data into separate columns.

Creating Subtotals

You can automatically insert subtotals into a sorted list without writing formulas:

1) Sort your data by the column you want to group (e.g. Category, Region, Product, Person, etc.).

2) Select the **Data** tab on the Ribbon, then click on the **Outline** button (on the right of the Ribbon) and select **Subtotal**. The "Subtotal" dialog box will be displayed.

3) From the **At each change in** drop-down list, select the column you sorted by.

4) From the **Use function** drop-down list, select the type of calculation you want for each group (e.g. Sum, Count, Average, etc.).

5) From the **Add subtotal to** list select the column(s) that you want to use for the calculation.

6) Click **OK**.

Excel will insert subtotal rows into your dataset and add outline controls on the left margin so you can expand/collapse detail, see only subtotals, or just the grand total.

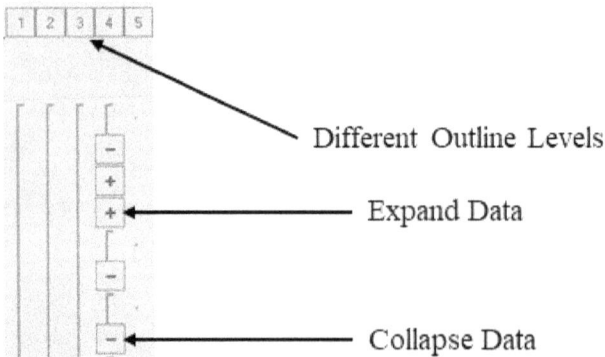

Different Outline Levels

Expand Data

Collapse Data

To remove the subtotals, select the **Data** tab on the Ribbon, then click on the **Outline** button (on the right of the Ribbon) and select **Subtotal**. From the "Subtotal" dialog box, click the **Remove All** button.

Formatting Subtotal Rows

When you use the Subtotal feature (refer to "*Creating Subtotals*"), Excel inserts subtotal rows into your list. If you manually format the whole range, the formatting will apply to every row – not just the subtotals.

However, if you collapse the outline using the outline buttons on the left of the worksheet, only the subtotal rows remain visible. Select the range of cells containing the subtotals and then press **F5**, click the **Special** button, select **Visible cells only**, and click **OK**.

You can now apply your formatting (e.g. bold, fill colour, font colour, borders, etc.). When you expand the outline again, only the subtotal rows will keep the special formatting you applied. This makes them much easier to spot.

Creating a PivotTable Quickly

A PivotTable is a versatile tool that allows you to summarise, analyse, and reorganise data from a table or range. It lets you explore the same data from different perspectives without altering the original source. With PivotTables, you can quickly group, filter, and calculate totals, averages, counts, and other summaries to uncover trends and insights.
The following steps describe how to quickly create a PivotTable.

1) Place the cell pointer anywhere within the range of data that you want to analyse.

2) Select the **Insert** tab on the Ribbon and from the **Tables** group, click the **PivotTable** button. The "PivotTable from table or range" dialog box will be displayed.

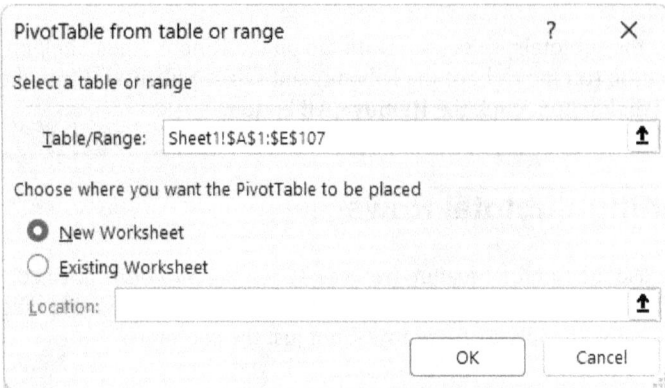

PivotTable from table or range   ?   ✕

Select a table or range

Table/Range: Sheet1!$A$1:$E$107

Choose where you want the PivotTable to be placed

◉ New Worksheet

○ Existing Worksheet

Location:

OK   Cancel

3) Select whether you'd like the PivotTable on a **New Worksheet** or on the **Existing Worksheet**.

4) Click **OK**.

A blank PivotTable layout is created, with the **PivotTable Fields** pane displayed on the right of the screen, allowing you to drag and drop fields into the Rows, Columns, Values, and Filters areas to build your report.

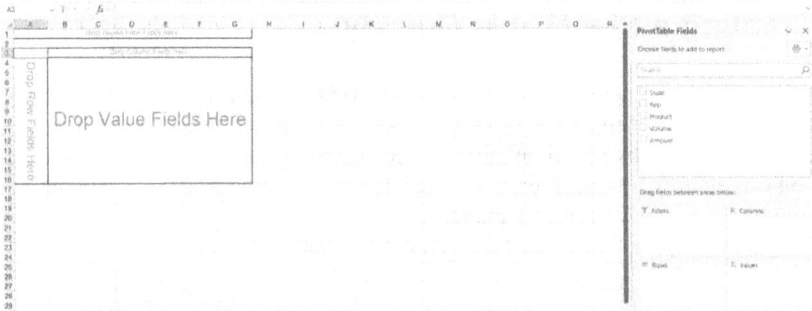

To create the PivotTable, drag and drop the field names from the PivotTable Fields pane into the Rows, Columns, Values, or Filters areas.

The following diagram shows the result with:
- the "Rep" field in the Rows area
- the "Product" field in the Columns area
- the "State" field in the Filter area
- the "Amount" field in the Values area

	A	B	C	D	E	F
1	State	(All)				
2						
3	Sum of Amount	Product				
4	Rep	Biscuits	Bread	Cakes	Pies	Grand Total
5	Beasley	$ 9,205.74		$ 42,223.64	$ 23,171.21	$ 74,600.59
6	Brunker	$ 35,262.03	$ 21,657.10	$ 39,638.99	$ 34,457.51	$131,015.63
7	Chan	$ 29,937.23	$ 26,472.11	$ 6,172.54	$ 25,340.36	$ 87,922.24
8	Crandell	$ 25,813.41	$ 9,692.79	$ 1,280.27	$ 16,830.48	$ 53,616.95
9	Curran	$ 10,025.23	$ 12,271.28	$ 125.17		$ 22,421.68
10	Galea	$ 22,431.55	$ 2,176.21	$ 34,978.55	$ 10,223.88	$ 69,810.19
11	Hassan	$ 18,426.91	$ 28,871.16	$ 22,777.13	$ 13,419.59	$ 83,494.79
12	Khan		$ 4,356.00	$ 34,444.65	$ 8,718.85	$ 47,519.50
13	O'Davis	$ 26,314.23	$ 11,569.36	$ 18,974.52	$ 43,657.19	$100,515.30
14	Taylor	$ 14,427.14	$ 7,566.09	$ 4,219.29	$ 5,692.67	$ 31,905.19
15	Wilson	$ 27,523.97		$ 2,906.54	$ 31,304.51	$ 61,735.02
16	Yousef	$ 14,088.15	$ 2,814.51	$ 11,912.55	$ 9,163.91	$ 37,979.12
17	Grand Total	$233,455.59	$127,446.61	$219,653.84	$221,980.16	$802,536.20

Drilling Down in PivotTables

After creating a PivotTable (refer to "*Creating a PivotTable Quickly*"), double-click on any of the values. Excel will create an additional sheet containing the full details of the summary value shown in the PivotTable.

In the following example, double-clicking on the active cell (D5) displays a summary of "Coffee" sales in the "South" region.

	A	B	C	D	E	F
1			Drop Report Filter Fields Here			
2						
3	Sum of Units Sold	Region				
4	Flavour	East	North	South	West	Grand Total
5	Butter Pecan	265785	348270	302445	412425	1328925
6	Chocolate	1044810	1182285	806520	1338090	4371705
7	Coffee	1503060	1622205	1356420	1750515	6232200
8	Pistachio	449085	494910	568230	650715	2162940
9	Strawberry	779025	696540	834015	934830	3244410
10	Vanilla	1273935	1127295	1072305	1328925	4802460
11	Vanilla Fudge	1383915	1338090	1118130	1466400	5306535
12	Grand Total	6699615	6809595	6058065	7881900	27449175

Double-clicking a value in a PivotTable

	A	B	C	D	E	F
1	Details for Sum of Units Sold - Flavour: Coffee, Region: South					
2						
3	Year	Flavour	Region	Units Sold	Sales	
4	2025	Coffee	South	224960	674880	
5	2025	Coffee	South	112480	337440	
6	2025	Coffee	South	182780	548340	
7	2025	Coffee	South	140600	421800	
8	2024	Coffee	South	236800	710400	
9	2024	Coffee	South	118400	355200	
10	2024	Coffee	South	192400	577200	
11	2024	Coffee	South	148000	444000	

Displays the underlying data on a new sheet

Disabling Drilldown in PivotTables

You can disable the PivotTable drill-down feature (refer to "*Drilling Down in PivotTables*") if you want to prevent users from seeing the detail behind a PivotTable.

1) Click anywhere inside the PivotTable.

2) On the Ribbon, go to the **PivotTable Analyze** tab.

3) In the **PivotTable** group, click the **Options** button. The "PivotTable Options" dialog box will be displayed.

4) Click on the **Data** tab.

5) Disable the **Enable Show Details** checkbox.

6) Click **OK**.

Group Dates in PivotTables

You can group dates together whether they're in the Rows or Columns area of your PivotTable.

Right-click on any date, and select the **Group** command from the shortcut menu. The "Grouping" dialog will be displayed, allowing you to group the dates by Days, Months, Quarters, Years, etc.

Excel will subtotal your data by the time periods you pick, making it easy to view monthly, quarterly, or yearly trends without changing your source data.

Filtering a PivotTable

You can use any field as a filter in a PivotTable.

Fields in the **Rows** or **Columns** areas can be filtered by clicking the drop-down arrow next to the field name in the PivotTable and selecting or clearing the checkboxes for the items you want to show.

Click the drop-down arrow next to the field name to select the items to filter

Fields in the Filters area can be filtered to display only selected items. By default, you can choose just one item, but you can enable multiple selections by enabling the **Select Multiple Items** checkbox. To apply a filter, click the drop-down arrow next to the field name above the PivotTable, select the item(s) you want to show, and click **OK**.

To filter multiple items from the field in the "Filter" area, enable the **Select Multiple Items** option

Using a PivotTable to Determine Percentage of a Total

In many spreadsheets you will be required to calculate the percentage of a total that a particular item represents. A PivotTable provides you with this functionality, without having to create a formula.

In the following example we want to calculate the percentage of total sales for each flavour of ice-cream.

	A	B
1	Flavour	Sales
2	Butter Pecan	29,000
3	Chocolate	114,000
4	Coffee	164,000
5	Pistachio	49,000
6	Strawberry	85,000
7	Vanilla	139,000
8	Vanilla Fudge	151,000
9	Butter Pecan	37,700
10	Chocolate	148,200
11	Coffee	213,200
12	Pistachio	63,700
13	Strawberry	110,500
14	Vanilla	180,700
15	Vanilla Fudge	196,300
16	Butter Pecan	23,200
17	Chocolate	91,200
18	Coffee	131,200
19	Pistachio	39,200
20	Strawberry	68,000

1) Create a PivotTable using the data that you want to summarise (refer to *"Creating a PivotTable Quickly"*).

2) Drag the field you want to summarise (in this example "Flavour") to the **Rows** area.

3) Drag the field containing the data (in this example "Sales") to the **Values** area.

4) Select any cell in the Values column.

5) On the Ribbon, go to the **PivotTable Analyze** tab, and in the **Active Field** group click **Field Settings**. The "Value Field Settings" dialog box will be displayed.

6) Click the **Show Values As** tab.

7) From the drop-down list, choose **% of Grand Total**.

Value Field Settings		□ X
Source Name: Sales		
Custom Name: Sum of Sales		
Summarize Values By	Show Values As	

Show values as

% of Grand Total ⌄

No Calculation
% of Grand Total
% of Column Total
% of Row Total
% Of
% of Parent Row Total

Number Format	OK	Cancel

8) Click **OK**.

The PivotTable will be arranged so that each item is shown with its percentage of the total of items.

	A	B
1		
2		
3	Sum of Sales	
4	Flavour ▾	Total
5	Butter Pecan	4.42%
6	Chocolate	17.37%
7	Coffee	24.99%
8	Pistachio	7.47%
9	Strawberry	12.95%
10	Vanilla	15.72%
11	Vanilla Fudge	17.07%
12	Grand Total	100.00%

Note: This information can be charted easily, by highlighting the data to chart and pressing **F11**.

Automate Report Creation with PivotTable Filter Pages

If you've added a field to the Filters area of your PivotTable, you can instantly create a new worksheet for each filter item using the **Show Report Filter Pages** command.

1) Click anywhere inside the PivotTable.

2) Select the **PivotTable Analyze** tab on the Ribbon and from the **PivotTable** group, click on the drop-down arrow next to the **Options** button.

3) Select the **Show Report Filter Pages** option and select the field that you want to expand and then click **OK**.

Select the drop-down arrow next to the "Options" button and select **Show Report Filter Pages**.

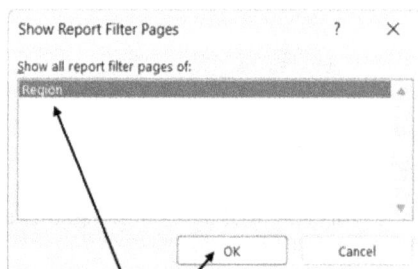

Select the field to expand and click **OK**. Excel will create a new sheet for each unique item in the selected field.

Excel will create a separate sheet for each item in that filter, with the PivotTable automatically set to display the corresponding data. This is a great way to generate individual reports, for example by region, department, or salesperson, without having to copy and filter manually.

Quick Analysis Tool

If you want fast insights from your data, use the **Quick Analysis Tool**. It lets you instantly apply charts, totals, tables, and conditional formatting to your data.

Simply highlight your data and press **CTRL+Q** to see suggestions for charts, totals, tables, and conditional formatting that you can apply immediately.

	A	B	C	D	E	F
1	**Region**	**Sales ($m)**				
2	January	251				
3	February	411				
4	March	354				
5	April	204				
6	May	285				
7	June	176				
8	July	80				
9	August	133				
10	September	305				
11	October	311				
12	November	380				
13	December	350				
14						
15						

Formatting	Charts	Totals	Tables	Sparklines
Data Bars	Color Scale	Icon Set	Greater Than	Top 10%	Clear Format

Conditional Formatting uses rules to highlight interesting data.

Removing Duplicates From a List

Excel's **Remove Duplicates** feature can be used to create a list of unique items from a list containing duplicate entries.

The following diagram shows the range used in this example (note the column heading is formatted differently from the rest of the column).

	A
1	**Fruits**
2	Apple
3	Cherry
4	Pear
5	Cherry
6	Plum
7	Apple
8	Apple
9	Pear
10	Apple
11	Pear

1) Click on a cell within the list of data that you want to analyse.

2) Go to the **Data** tab on the Ribbon.

3) In the **Data Tools** group, click the **Remove Duplicates** button. The "Remove Duplicates" dialog box will be displayed.

4) If your data has headings, ensure the **My data has headers** option is enabled.

5) Select the column(s) you want Excel to check for duplicates.

6) Click **OK**.

Excel will remove the duplicates and tell you how many were removed and how many remain.

The following diagram shows the results of this process using this example.

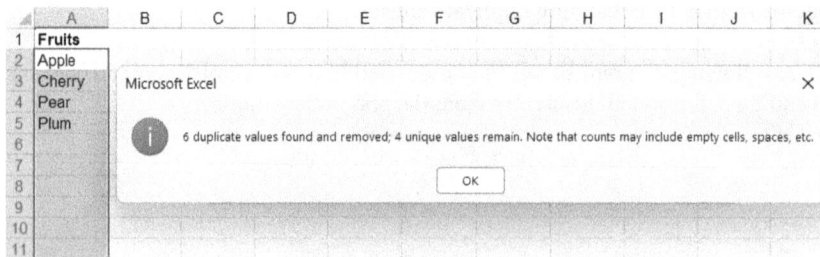

Extracting Unique Items from a List

Excel's **Advanced Filter** can be used to extract a list of unique items from a list containing duplicate entries.

In the following example, we want to extract the unique paint colours, and list them starting in cell D2.

	A
1	**Paint Colours**
2	Ocean Mist
3	Golden Wheat
4	Golden Wheat
5	Charcoal Slate
6	Golden Wheat
7	Charcoal Slate
8	Sunset Coral
9	Ocean Mist
10	Golden Wheat
11	Sunset Coral
12	Sunset Coral
13	Ocean Mist
14	Golden Wheat
15	Ocean Mist
16	Charcoal Slate
17	Golden Wheat
18	Sunset Coral
19	Ocean Mist

1)   Ensure the cell pointer is located in the range of cells that you want to extract the unique entries from (in this example cells A1 to A19).

2)   Go to the **Data** tab on the Ribbon.

3)   In the **Sort & Filter** group, click on the **Advanced** button. The "Advanced Filter" dialog box will be displayed.

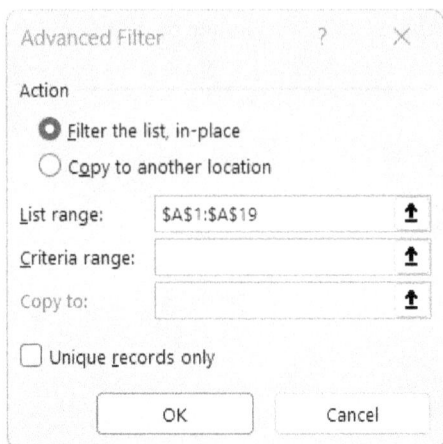

4) Select the **Copy to another location** option.

5) In the **Copy** to field, select where you want to copy the results to (in this example D2).

6) Enable the **Unique records only** option.

7) Click **OK**. Excel will copy just the unique items to the location you chose, leaving the original list unchanged.

	A	B	C	D
1	**Paint Colours**			**Paint Colours**
2	Ocean Mist			Ocean Mist
3	Golden Wheat			Golden Wheat
4	Golden Wheat			Charcoal Slate
5	Charcoal Slate			Sunset Coral
6	Golden Wheat			
7	Charcoal Slate			
8	Sunset Coral			

CHARTS AND DRAWING TOOLS

Quickly Creating New Charts

To quickly create a chart on its own sheet, highlight the data that you want to chart and press **F11**. If Excel can interpret the data correctly, a new chart will be created on a separate sheet of the workbook. The chart created is the default column chart.

If Excel cannot interpret the data correctly, the **Insert Chart** dialog box will open so you can choose the chart type, data series, and layout.

Note: You can use **ALT+F1** to create a new chart on the current worksheet.

Creating Charts Without Selecting Ranges

Excel allows you to create a chart without having to first select the data. With the cell pointer located in a data range, pressing **F11** or **ALT+F1** (see *Quickly Creating New Charts*) creates a chart based on the range bounded by blank cells around the data area (similar to the way Excel handles lists for sorting and filtering).

For example, pressing **F11** or **ALT+F1** with the cell pointer positioned as shown below, Excel would create a chart based on the data in cells A1 to C7.

	A	B	C
1		US	ASIA
2	Electronics	752	716
3	Automotive	187	506
4	Software	550	407
5	Textiles	562	114
6	Services	620	290
7	Other	586	155

Moving a Chart's Location

Excel charts can appear either on a chart sheet or as an embedded object on a worksheet. To quickly move a chart between these two locations, ensure that the chart you want to move is selected, and then from the **Chart Design** tab on the Ribbon, click the **Move Chart** command.

Move Chart	? ✕

Choose where you want the chart to be placed:

⦿ New sheet: Chart1

○ Object in: Sheet1 ⌄

OK   Cancel

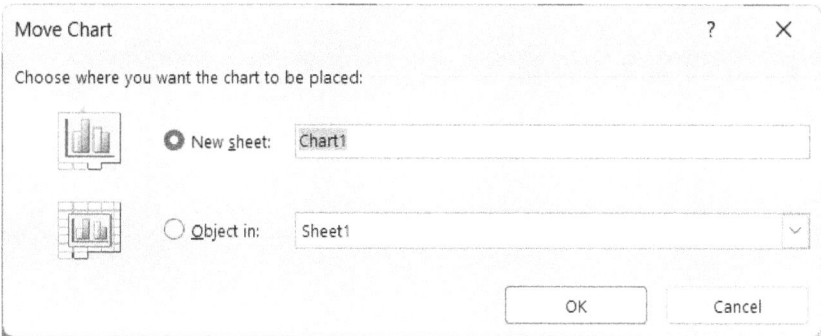

Selecting Different Chart Elements

It can sometimes be tricky to click exactly the right element on a chart (for example, a single data series, axis label, or plot area). Here are two ways to select chart elements precisely.

1)   Chart element tooltips

When you hover the mouse pointer over different parts of a chart, Excel displays a small tooltip identifying that element (e.g. Chart Area, Series "Sales", Axis Title). This helps confirm what will be selected if you click on an element.

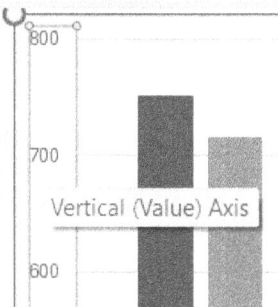

2)   Chart Elements drop-down

Select the chart, then go to the **Format** tab on the Ribbon. In the **Current Selection** group, use the **Chart Elements** drop-down list to pick the exact element you want to work with.

| File | Home | Insert | Page Layout | Formulas | Data | Review | View | Automate | Help | Acrobat | Chart Design | Format |

Vertical (Value) Axis Ma

Chart Area

Horizontal (Category) Axis

Legend

Plot Area

Vertical (Value) Axis

Vertical (Value) Axis Major Gridlines

Series "US"

Series "ASIA"

Shape Outline ˅

Shape Effects ˅

Shape Styles

WordArt Styles

800

700

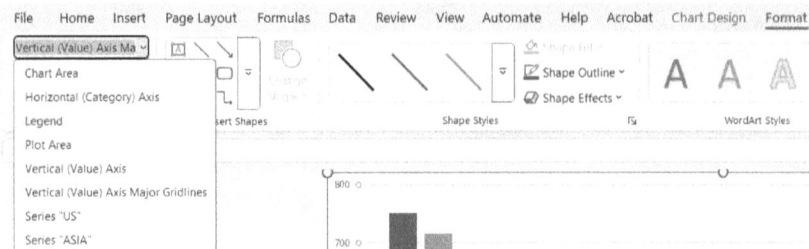

Displaying a Data Table with a Chart

Excel allows you to display a data table beneath a chart, showing the values used to create it.

1) Click the chart to select it and then select the **Chart Design** tab on the Ribbon.

2) Click the **Add Chart Element** button and select **Data Table**.

3) Choose one of the following:

With Legend Keys — displays the series name, legend keys, and data values.

No Legend Keys — displays just the data values and series names without the colour-coded keys.

Note: If you choose With Legend Keys, you can remove the separate chart legend, as the keys appear in the table.

To adjust the table's text size, select the table, then change the font size from the **Home** tab.

Data tables are only available for Column, Bar, Line, Area, and Stock chart types.

You can also use the Chart Elements button (+) that appears to the right of the chart to quickly add a Data Table to the chart.

	Chart Elements		
	☑ Axes		
	☐ Axis Titles		
	☐ Chart Title		
	☐ Data Labels		
	☐ Data Table >	With Legend Keys	
	☐ Error Bars	No Legend Keys	
	☑ Gridlines	More Options...	
	☐ Legend		
	☐ Trendline		

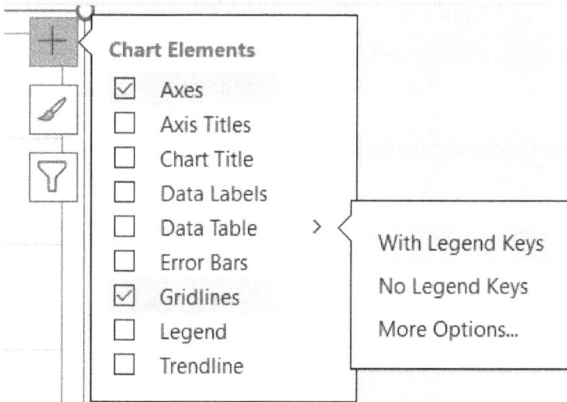

Rotating Data in a Pie Chart

By default, Excel plots the data series in a pie chart in the same order as the source data on the worksheet. However, you can change the position of the slices by rotating the pie.

1) Click on the pie chart to select it.

2) Right-click on any slice and choose **Format Data Series**. The "Format Data Series" pane appears on the right of the screen.

3) Adjust the **Angle of first slice** setting by typing a number or using the up/down arrows.

As you change the value, the position of the slices rotates around the circle. For example, setting it to 90° will move the first slice to the right side of the chart.

Creating a Combo Chart

Sometimes it's useful to mix chart types – for example, showing one data series as a line and another as columns.

Method 1 – Using the Combo Chart Feature

1) Select the range of data that you want to chart.

2) Select the **Insert** tab on the Ribbon and from the **Charts** group click on the ▥ ˅ **Insert Combo Chart** button.

3) Choose one of the preset column types or a **Custom Combination Chart**.

4) If you selected "**Custom Combination Chart**" in the previous step, use the dialog box to select a chart type for each data series (e.g. *Clustered Column* for one, *Line* for another) and if required, enable the **Secondary Axis** for a series (useful when the scales are very different), then click **OK**.

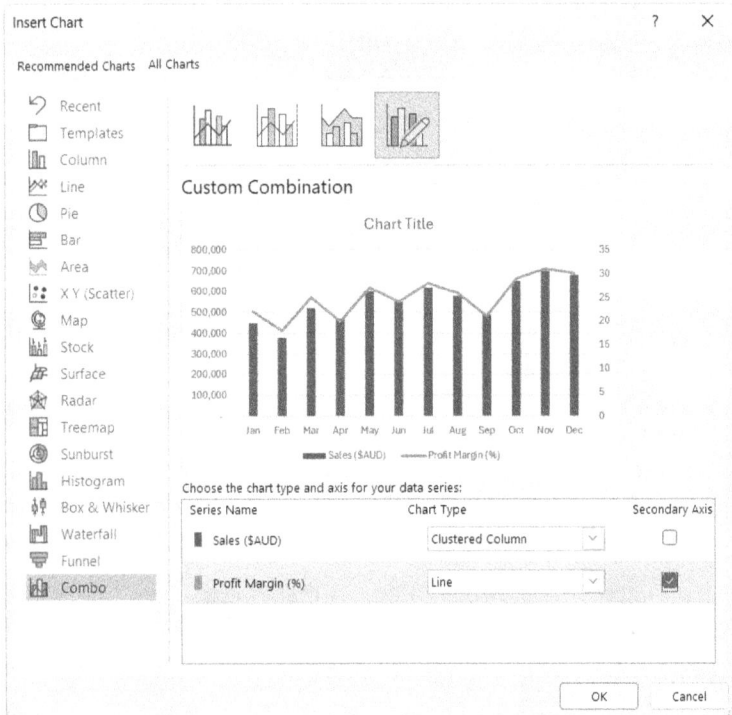

Method 2 – Converting one series in an existing chart

1) Create a standard chart (e.g. clustered column).

2) Click the chart to select it, then select the specific data series you want to change (refer to "*Selecting Different Chart Elements*").

3) Select the **Chart Design** tab on the Ribbon and then click on the **Change Chart Type** button.

4) Choose **Combo** from the list of chart types and then click on the **Custom Combination** option.

5) Assign chart types for each series, enable the **Secondary Axis** if required, then click **OK**.

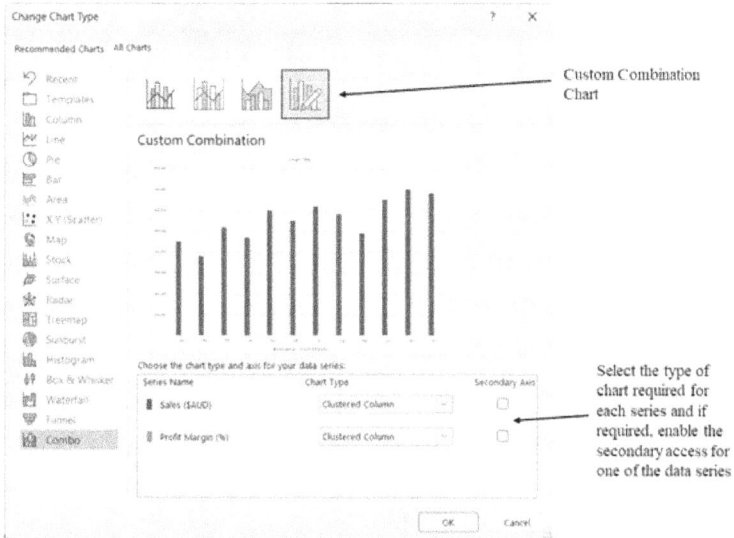

Creating Picture Charts

You can create a chart that uses a picture (graphic) in place of a column to represent the chart data. This can either be applied to all the columns in the chart, or to an individual column.

1) Click once on the chart to select it and then click once on the column (or series) you want to format. To format only one column, click the series once, then click that specific column again to select just that data point (refer to *"Selecting Different Chart Elements"*).

2) Right-click the selected column or series and choose **Format Data Series** (or **Format Data Point** if only one column is selected).

3) In the Format Data Series (or Data Point) pane, click **Fill & Line** (the paint bucket icon).

4) Click on the **Fill** drop-down option and then select **Picture or texture fill**.

5) In the **Picture source** area, click the **Insert...** button and then the appropriate option for the source of the picture you want to use.

Format Data Series   ∨

∨ Series Options

─────────────

∨ **Fill**

○ No fill
○ Solid fill
○ Gradient fill
◉ Picture or texture fill
○ Pattern fill
○ Automatic
☐ Invert if negative
☐ Vary colors by point

Picture source

[Insert...] [Clipboard]

Insert Pictures

From a File
Browse files on your computer or local network

Stock Images
Unleash your imagination with premium content from the stock image library

Online Pictures
Search images from online sources like Bing, Flickr or OneDrive

From Icons
Search the icon collection

Select **Fill & Line** then **Picture or texture fill** and then click the **Insert...** button. You will be asked for the source of the picture you'd like to use.

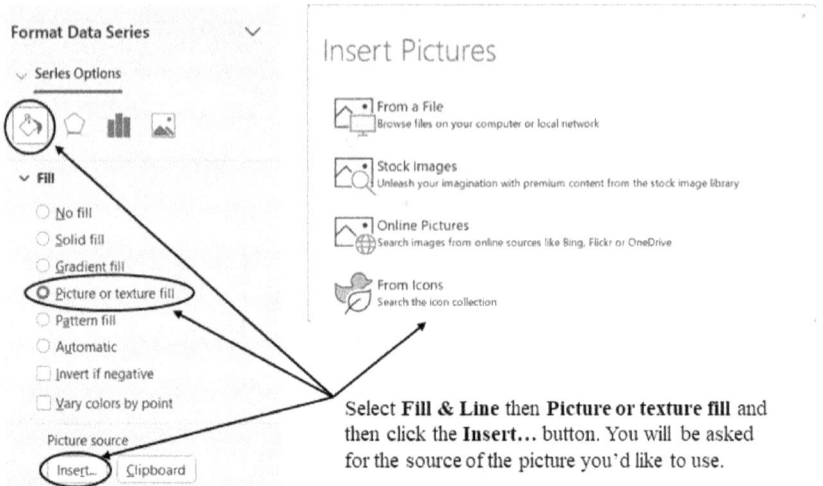

6) Select the picture that you want to use for the selected series (or column).

7) If necessary, choose one of the following options to adjust how the picture appears in the column:

Stack

Repeats the picture for each unit of value in the column. The more the value, the more times the image stacks.

Stretch

Stretches a single instance of the picture to fill the entire column, regardless of value.

Stack and Scale with

Stacks the picture, but scales it to represent the value proportionally. For example, a value of 50 will display half the number of pictures compared to 100.

A sample picture chart is shown below.

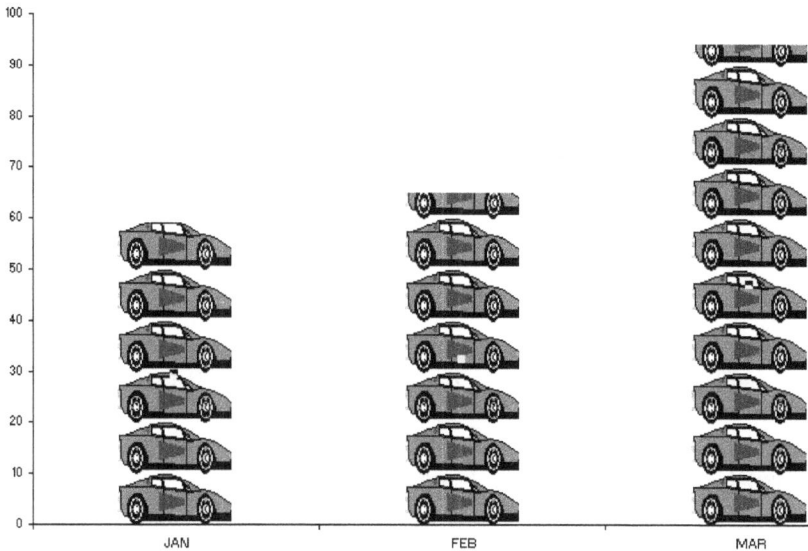

Note: You can also create a picture chart by copying a graphic to the clipboard, selecting the series (or column) that you want to apply it to and using the Paste command to add it to the chart. To adjust the stacking/scaling of the image, double-click on the column(s) and adjust the options from the **Format Data Series** pane.

Copying Chart Formatting

If you have refined the appearance of one chart and want to apply the same look to others, there is no need to recreate everything. You can simply copy the formatting.

1) Click the formatted chart (make sure the whole chart area is selected).

2) Press **CTRL+C.**

3) Select the target chart (again ensure you have selected the chart area).

4) Select the **Home** tab on the Ribbon, and from the **Clipboard** group, click the drop-down arrow under the **Paste** button and select **Paste Special**. The "Paste Special" dialog box will be displayed, as shown below.

Paste Special	?	X

Paste

◉ All
◯ Formats
◯ Formulas

OK	Cancel

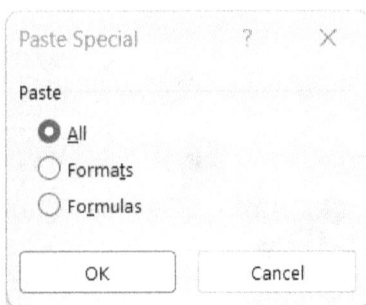

5) Select the **Format** option and click **OK**. The second chart instantly adopts all the colours, fonts, and style choices from the first.

Creating a Custom Chart Type

Excel allows you to create your own custom chart types that can be reused when creating new charts in any workbook. This is useful if you regularly apply the same formatting, layout, and other chart options, saving you from making the same changes each time.

1) Create a chart and apply all the formatting you want to use in the chart template (e.g. colours, fonts, labels, gridlines, and effects).

2) Right-click in the Chart Area and select **Save as Template**.

3) Type a name for your template and click **Save**.

Note: The template is saved with a .crtx extension in the \Templates\Charts folder.

Once you have saved a custom chart template you can use it as the starting point for new charts.

1) Select the data you want to use for the chart.

2) From the **Insert** tab on the Ribbon, in the **Charts** group, click the **Recommended Charts** button. The "Insert Chart" dialog box will be displayed.

3) Click on the **All Charts** tab and then click on the **Templates** option.

4) Select your saved chart template from the gallery.

5) Click **OK** to create the chart and then make an additional adjustments to formatting or layout if needed.

Using the Range Finder in Embedded Charts

Excel highlights the ranges used in a chart embedded on a worksheet, in a similar way to the method used to highlight cells or ranges in a formula you are editing (refer to "*Modifying a Range Reference in a Formula*").

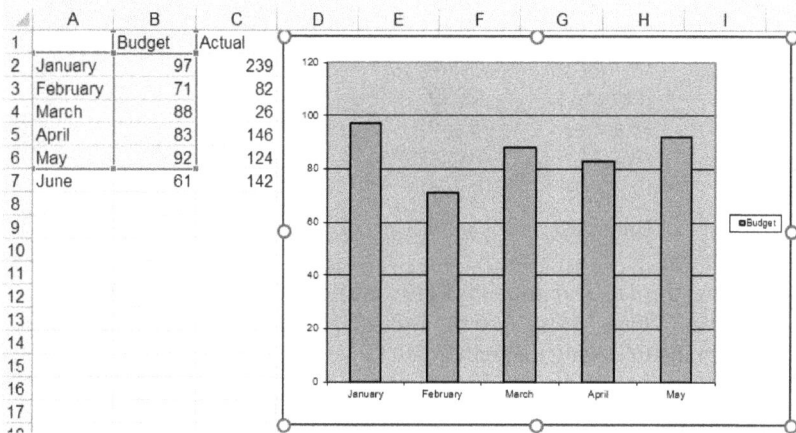

The chart ranges can be adjusted by dragging the border of the range to include or exclude data from the chart.

Multi-Level Category Axis

You can create charts with multiple items on the category axis (x-axis).

The data shown below contains sales information for several different products in several different states.

	A	B	C
1	**State**	**Product**	**Sales**
2	NSW	Oranges	1887
3		Limes	2462
4		Lemons	1000
5		Bananas	1956
6	QLD	Oranges	2111
7		Limes	2548
8		Lemons	1340
9		Bananas	2999
10	VIC	Oranges	2852
11		Limes	3685
12		Lemons	2782
13		Bananas	3459

Highlighting the data and pressing **F11** to create a chart (refer to *"Quickly Creating New Charts"*) results in the two categories being used on the x-axis as shown in the following diagram.

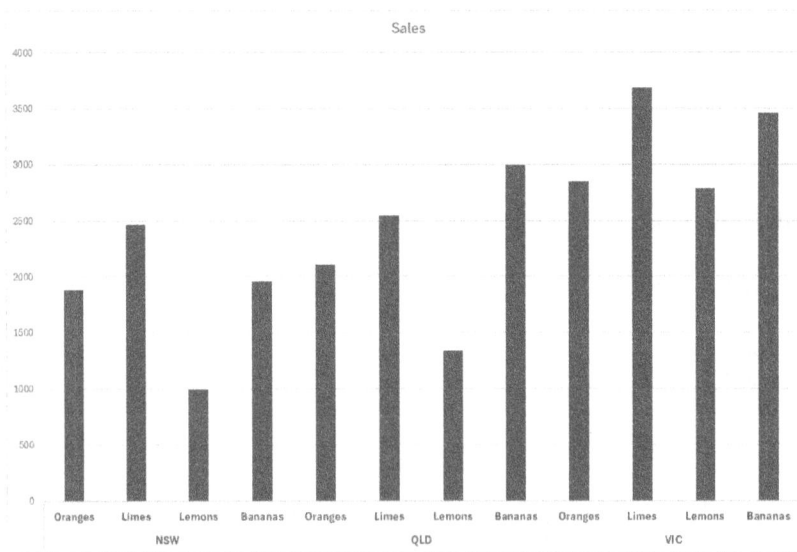

Note: This same technique works with any nested categories (e.g., Region → State, or Department → Team). Just place the broader category in the first column and the detail in the second, and Excel will build multi-level labels on the axis automatically.

Quick Forecasting Using Charts

You can add trendlines to a chart to show current and future trends for the data that you are charting.

1) Create a chart using the data you want to analyse.

2) Right-click on the data series that you want to forecast and select the **Add Trendline** from the shortcut menu. A simple, linear trendline is added to the chart.

3) In the "Format Trendline" pane, under **Trendline Options**, select the type of trendline you want (e.g. Exponential, Linear, Moving Average, etc.).

4) To forecast forward or backward, in the **Forecast** section, enter the number of periods (months, years, etc.) in the **Forward** or **Backward** boxes. A trendline with a forecast is inserted in the chart, as shown below.

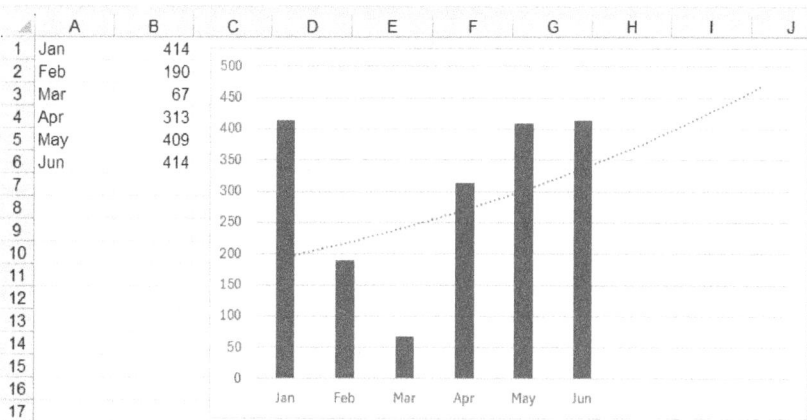

Displaying Cell Contents in a Chart Text Box

You can display the contents of a worksheet cell on a chart by inserting a text box linked to that cell. This is useful for showing dynamic information (e.g. the result of a formula) that updates automatically when the cell changes.

1) Create the chart where you want the linked text to appear.

2) Select the **Format** tab on the Ribbon then click the drop-down arrow in the **Insert Shapes** area and select the **Text Box** shape.

3) Click and drag on the chart to draw the text box in the desired position.

4) Click on the outside border of the text box to select it.

5) Click in the Formula Bar, type an equals sign (=) to start a formula, then click the cell you want to link to and press **Enter**.

The text box now displays the content of the linked cell. If the cell value changes, the text in the chart will update automatically.

Handling Missing Data with Charts

When a chart is created and there are empty cells in the data range used to create the chart, the default option is to leave a gap in the chart to cater for the missing data, as shown below.

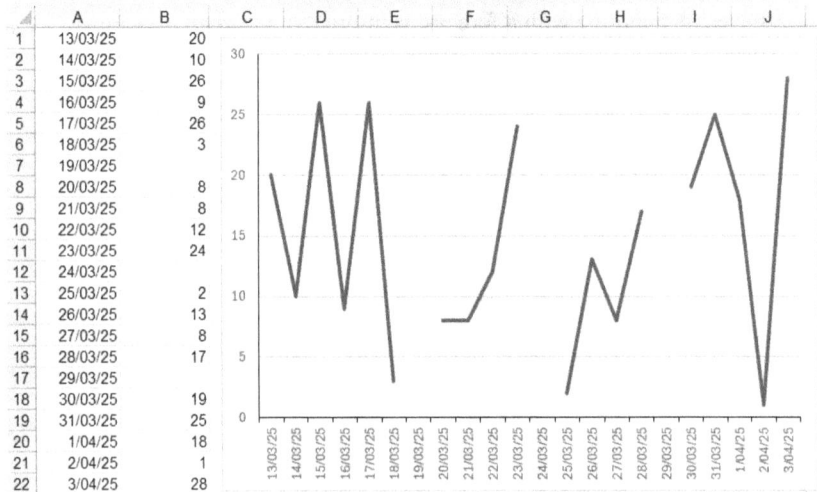

Excel provides some additional options for handling blank cells in the chart's data range.

1) Ensure the chart is selected.

2) Select the **Chart Design** tab on the Ribbon, and in the **Data** group, click **Select Data**. The "Select Data Source" dialog box will be displayed.

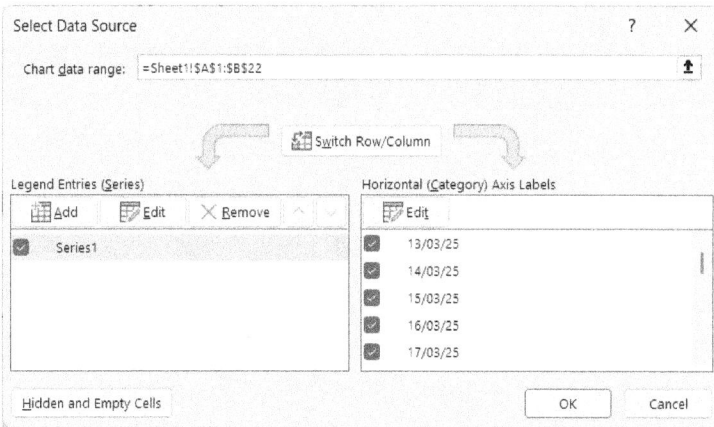

Select Data Source

Chart data range: =Sheet1!$A$1:$B$22

Switch Row/Column

Legend Entries (Series)

Add   Edit   Remove

☑   Series1

Horizontal (Category) Axis Labels

Edit

☑   13/03/25
☑   14/03/25
☑   15/03/25
☑   16/03/25
☑   17/03/25

Hidden and Empty Cells   OK   Cancel

3) Click the **Hidden and Empty Cells** button.

4) Select the required option from the **Show empty cells as** command;

    Gaps — leaves a break where the blank cell occurs.

    Zero — treats blank cells as if they contain the value zero.

    Connect data points with line — estimates the missing value and connects the line between surrounding data points (interpolation).

5) Click **OK** twice to apply the setting.

The following chart displays the **Connect data points with line** option.

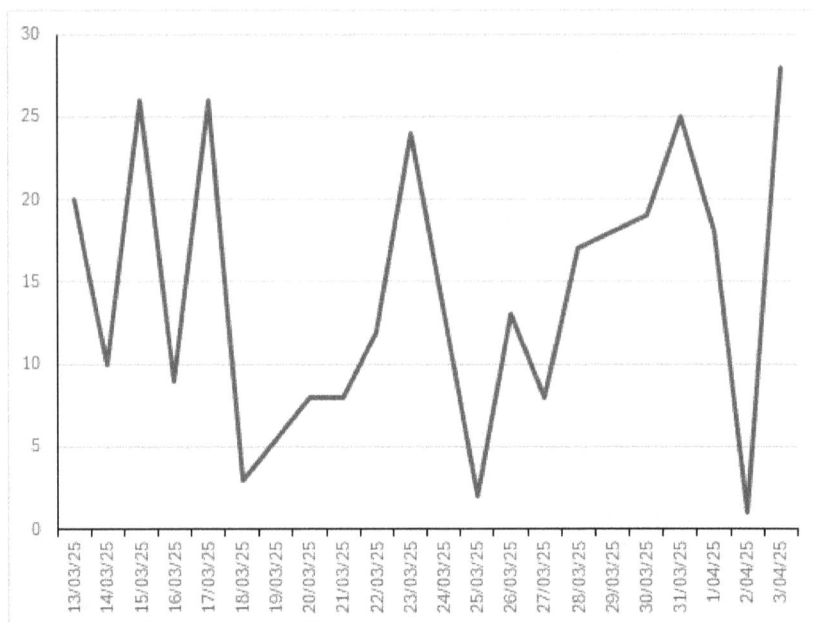

Note: Entering the formula =**NA()** in the blank cells causes Excel to interpolate the data, without needing to adjust the chart options.

Displaying Large Values on the Chart's Axis

When you plot large values on a chart, the y-axis can become difficult to read, even when formatted with thousands separators. A quick change to the format of the axis can make the values on it more legible.

1) Right-click on the chart's y-axis and select **Format Axis.** The "Format Axis" pane will be displayed.

2) In the "Format Axis" pane, expand the **Axis Options** section if needed, and in the **Display units** area, choose a suitable unit from the drop-down list (e.g. Thousands, Millions, Billions).

Format Axis ⌄

⌄ **Axis Options**   Text Options

◇   ⬠   ⊞   ◨

Bounds

Minimum	0.0	Auto
Maximum	4.0E7	Auto

Units

		None
		Hundreds
Major	5.0E6	Thousands
		10000
Minor	1.0E6	100000
Horizontal axis crosses		Millions
⦿ Automatic		10000000
◯ Axis value		100000000
◯ Maximum axis valu		Billions
		Trillions
Display units	None	⌄

☐ Show display units label on chart

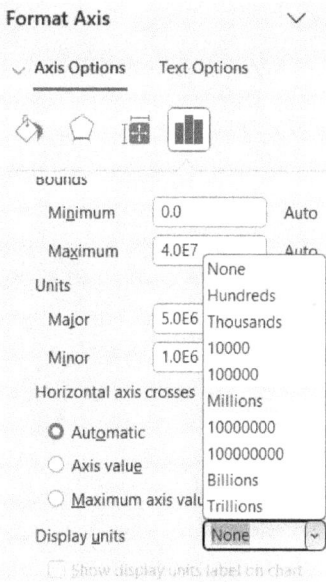

3)   You can also enable or disable the **Show display units label on chart** option as desired.

Creating a PivotChart

A PivotChart report is an interactive chart that provides a graphical analysis of data from existing lists, databases, and PivotTable reports.

After you create a PivotChart report, you can view different levels of detail or reorganise the layout of the chart by dragging fields and items around or by displaying and hiding items in the field drop-down lists.

The following steps describe the process of creating a PivotChart report.

1)   Select any cell in the range or table containing your data.

2)   Select the **Insert** tab on the Ribbon and in the **Charts** group, click the **PivotChart** button. The "Create PivotChart" dialog box is displayed.

Create PivotChart — □ ×

Choose the data that you want to analyze

◉ Select a table or range

Table/Range: 'Sales Data'!$A$1:$E$225   ⬆

○ Use an external data source

Choose Connection...

Connection name:

○ Use this workbook's Data Model

Choose where you want the PivotChart to be placed

◉ New Worksheet

○ Existing Worksheet

Location: ⬆

Choose whether you want to analyze multiple tables

☐ Add this data to the Data Model

OK   Cancel

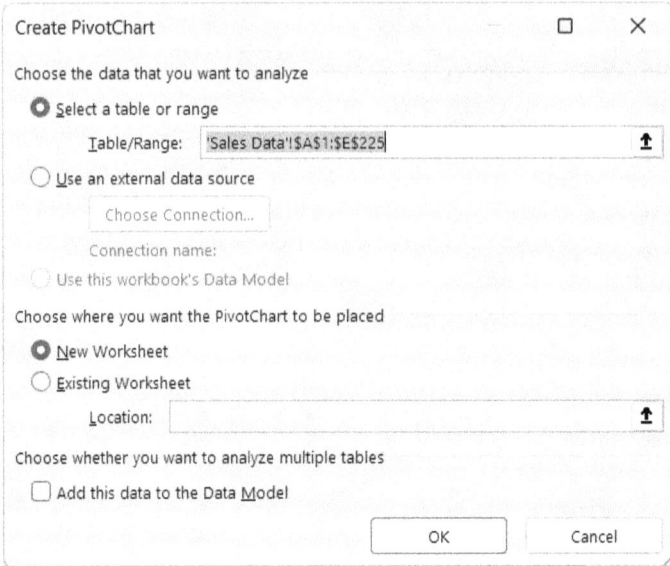

3) Verify the data range to be used and select where to place the PivotChart – either in a **New Worksheet** or on the **Existing Worksheet** and click **OK**. The "PivotTable Fields" pane appears.

4) Drag the fields you want into the Axis (Categories), Legend (Series), and Values areas to build the chart.

PivotChart Fields ∨ ✕

Choose fields to add to report: ⚙ ⌄

Search 🔍

☑ **Year**
☐ Flavour
☑ **Region**
☑ **Units Sold**
☐ Sales

Drag fields between areas below:

⊤ Filters

▥ Legend (Series)

Year ⌄

▦ Axis (Categories)

Region ⌄

∑ Values

Sum of Units Sold ⌄

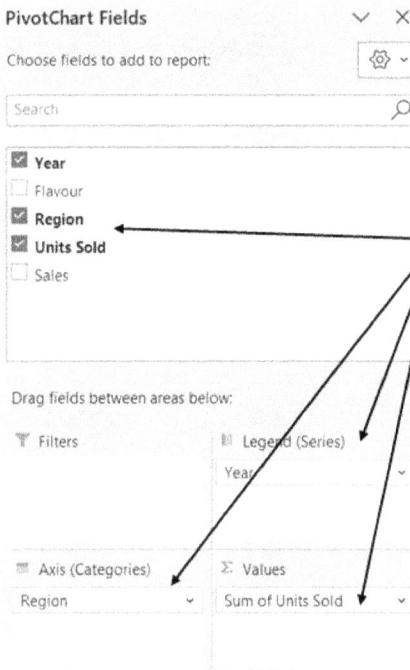

Drag the fields from the top section of the "PivotChart Fields" pane to the:
Legend (Series)
Axis (Category) and
Values
areas at the bottom of the pane

5)   Use the drop-down arrows on the chart to filter or hide items as required.

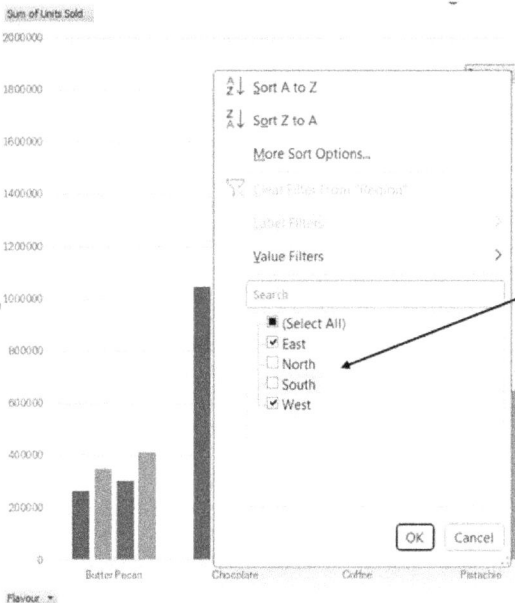

Use the drop-down arrows on the chart to filter or hide items as required.

Note: Any changes you make to the corresponding PivotTable are automatically reflected in the PivotChart, and changes you make to the PivotChart (such as filtering or rearranging fields) are also applied to the PivotTable.

Removing PivotChart Field Buttons

When you create a PivotChart (refer to "*Creating a PivotChart*"), Excel automatically adds grey buttons representing the fields used to create it.

Whilst these buttons are useful when creating the PivotChart, you may not require them afterwards, especially when you are formatting and printing the chart.

You can easily toggle the display of the field buttons on a PivotChart.

1) Click anywhere on the PivotChart to select it.

2) Select the **PivotChart Analyze** tab on the Ribbon and in the **Show/Hide** group, click on the **Field Buttons** button.

Visualising Data on a Map

Excel allows you to visualise location-based data with the **Filled Map** chart type. When your dataset includes geographic fields such as country, state, or region names (for example, New South Wales or New Zealand), you can plot values against those areas to highlight geographic patterns and trends.

1) Highlight a data range that includes locations (such as countries, states, or regions) and a corresponding value for each location.

2) Select the **Insert** tab on the Ribbon and from the **Charts** group, click on the **Maps** button and select **Filled Map**.

Excel will generate a map with shaded regions showing your values. You can adjust colours, labels, and titles, etc. in a similar way to other types of charts.

	A	B	C	D	E	F	G	H	I	J
1	State / Territory	Labour Force Participation Rate (%)				Chart Title				
2	Northern Territory	72.2								
3	Australian Capital Territory	71.1								
4	Western Australia	69.1								
5	Victoria	67.4								
6	Queensland	66.9								
7	New South Wales	66.2								
8	South Australia	63.5								
9	Tasmania	60.3								
10										
11										
12										
13										

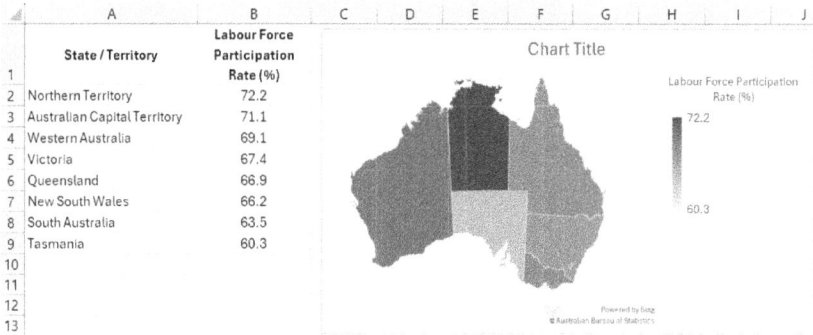

Drawing Perfect Shapes in Excel

You can create "perfect" shapes in Excel by holding down the **SHIFT** key while drawing shapes from the Insert tab.

For example, using **SHIFT** with the;
- **Oval** button creates a circle.
- **Rectangle** button creates a square.
- **Line** and **Arrow** buttons creates perfect horizontal and vertical lines, as well as lines in 15-degree increments from their starting points.

You can also hold **SHIFT** while drawing other shapes (e.g. triangles, stars) to keep them proportional.

Snap Objects to Cell Borders

Sometimes you may want an object such as a chart, shape or text box to match the exact dimensions of a cell range.

To do this, hold down the **ALT** key while drawing or resizing the object. The edges of the object will automatically snap to the cell borders for precise alignment.

PRINTING

Controlling Page Breaks in Page Break Preview Mode

An easy way to adjust page breaks is to use Excel's Page Break Preview feature.

1) Select the **View** tab on the Ribbon, and from the **Workbook Views** group, click **Page Break Preview**.

2) In Page Break Preview mode blue lines show automatic page breaks. You can click and drag these lines to adjust page boundaries. Excel will automatically change the print scaling factor when you do this.

3) To insert or remove a manual page break, right-click a cell and use the **Insert Page Break** or **Remove Page Break** options.

4) You can also choose to **Reset All Page Breaks** or **Set Print Area** from the same shortcut menu.

5) To exit Page Break Preview mode, select the **View** tab on the Ribbon and from the **Workbook Views** group click **Normal**.

Removing Manual Page Breaks

If your worksheet is cluttered with page breaks you've added manually, you can clear them all in one step.

Click the **Select All** button in the top-left corner of the sheet (the little triangle between row numbers and column letters). Then select the **Page Layout** tab on the Ribbon, and from the **Page Setup** category select **Breaks**, and then the **Reset All Page Breaks** command.

Excel removes every manual page break at once, saving you from deleting them one by one.

Using an Ampersand in Headers and Footers

In Excel, the ampersand character (&) is used as part of the codes that insert dynamic information in a header or footer (e.g. &[Page] for page numbers). Because of this, typing a single ampersand in a header or footer will not display as expected – Excel treats it as the start of a code and drops it from the printed result.

For example: Typing "Sales & Marketing" will print as "Sales Marketing" (i.e. the & disappears).

To display an actual ampersand character, you need to type it twice, for example: Typing "Sales && Marketing" will print as "Sales & Marketing".

Displaying Row and Column Headings on a Printout

When auditing spreadsheets or checking for errors in formulas, printing the worksheet with row numbers and column letters can make tracing formulas easier.

1) Select the **Page Layout** tab on the Ribbon.

2) In the **Sheet Options** group, under **Headings**, enable the **Print** checkbox.

Combining this feature with printing the **Gridlines** (also in the **Sheet Options** group on the **Page Layout** tab of the Ribbon) and with the formulas displayed (refer to "*Viewing Formulas*") produces a printout that can be effectively used to audit or troubleshoot formulas.

	A	B	C
1			
2			
3		Jan	Feb
4	Sales	1000	=B4+($C$10*B4)
5	Cost	=$C$11*B4	=$C$11*C4
6	Profit	=B4-B5	=C4-C5
7	Expenses	=$C$12*B4	=$C$12*C4
8	Income	=B6-B7	=C6-C7

Setting Print Ranges and Titles Using Named Ranges

You can quickly set what prints by naming a range, without needing to open the Page Setup dialog. This works because Excel recognises a specially reserved range name, **Print_Area**, and automatically treats that named range as the area to print.

To set the print area:

1) Select the cells you want to print.

2) Click in the **Name Box** (to the left of the formula bar).

3) Type **Print_Area** and press **Enter**.

Select the area to print and type
"Print_Area" in the Name Box

Print_Area		fx					
	A	B	C	D	E	F	G
1		January	February	March	April	May	June
2	Product 1	195	507	800	536	534	387
3	Product 2	640	678	789	294	421	824
4	Product 3	947	160	786	814	388	516
5	Product 4	829	964	335	788	145	679
6	Product 5	558	115	391	734	598	183
7	Product 6	130	125	770	843	600	487
8	Product 7	804	489	561	896	711	642
9	Product 8	796	637	744	961	761	841
10	Product 9	952	713	959	704	718	504
11	Product 10	549	700	949	599	142	388
12	Product 11	524	358	404	248	613	708
13	Product 12	586	382	304	172	522	641
14	Product 13	152	371	916	462	505	541
15	Product 14	994	908	386	572	320	469
16	Product 15	253	292	977	623	910	837

You can also define rows or columns to repeat on every printed page by using another reserved range name, **Print_Titles**. This ensures that key headings (like column labels or row titles) remain visible across multiple pages.

1) Select the rows and/or columns you want repeated on each page.

2) Click in the **Name Box**.

3) Type **Print_Titles** and press **Enter**.

Printing or Substituting Error Values

When printing a spreadsheet, you can elect to print error values as they appear on your worksheet, or you can replace each of the error values with a predefined character, such as a blank space or a dash, in the printed output.

Error values include #NUM!, #DIV/0!, #REF!, #N/A, #VALUE!, #NAME?, and #NULL!.

1) Select the **Page Layout** tab on the Ribbon.

2) In the **Page Setup** group, click the Page Setup launcher arrow (located in the bottom-right corner of the group). The "Page Setup" dialog box will be displayed.

3) Click on the **Sheet** tab, and from the **Cell errors as** drop-down list, choose one of the following options:

   Displayed (shows the actual error value)

   Blank (prints as empty cells)

   - - (dash)

   #N/A

4) Click **OK** to apply the setting.

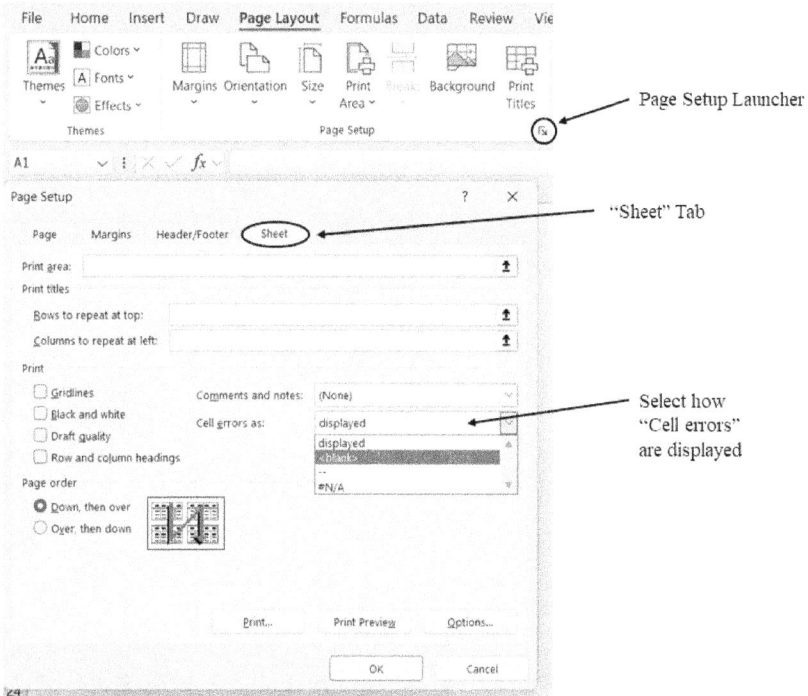

Page Setup Launcher

"Sheet" Tab

Select how
"Cell errors"
are displayed

This setting applies only to printing – the error values still appear in the worksheet itself.

MISCELLANEOUS

Using the Name Box

The Name Box (shown below) can be used to quickly create range names for use in formulas (see "*Using Range Names in Formulas*"). It also provides a fast way to navigate between named ranges in a workbook.

A1	⌄

To create (define) a new range name, highlight the cell(s) that you want to name and then click once in the Name Box. Type in the name that you want to use (range names cannot include spaces) and then press **ENTER**.

To move quickly to a named area of the spreadsheet, click on the drop-down arrow located next to the Name Box. A list of defined range names will be displayed. Clicking on a range name will take the cell pointer to that area of the spreadsheet.

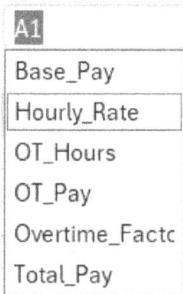

A1
Base_Pay
Hourly_Rate
OT_Hours
OT_Pay
Overtime_Factc
Total_Pay

Creating a List of Range Names

When working with named ranges, it's often useful to have a list showing the names in use and the cell references they refer to. This can help with auditing, documentation, and troubleshooting. The following steps describe how to create a table listing range names and their corresponding cell references.

1) Move to a blank area of your worksheet (or insert a new sheet) where you want the list to appear.

2) Press **F3**. The "Paste Name" dialog box will be displayed.

3) Click the **Paste List** button. The list of named ranges will be inserted, with the range names in the first column and the corresponding cell references in the second column.

4) Adjust the column widths (e.g., by double-clicking the right edge of the column headers) so that all details are visible.

I	J
Base_Pay	='Payroll Calculations'!$C$4:$C$7
Hourly_Rate	='Payroll Calculations'!$B$4:$B$7
OT_Hours	='Payroll Calculations'!$D$4:$D$7
OT_Pay	='Payroll Calculations'!$E$4:$E$7
Overtime_Factor	='Payroll Calculations'!$B$11
Total_Pay	='Payroll Calculations'!$F$4:$F$7

Preventing Errors with Data Validation

A simple data entry error can cause havoc with a spreadsheet. Excel's **Data Validation** feature helps prevent many common errors by restricting what can be entered into a cell.

Valid data may include:

*   Values within a range (e.g. between 50 and 200, or less than 5000)

*   Entries from a list (e.g. select a department from a drop-down list)

*   Values based on a formula (e.g. a number that ensures the total in a range stays below a set amount)

In the following example, the data validation feature is used to ensure that a valid department is entered in cells B2:B7 and that the hours worked entered in cells C2:C7 are less than 40.

	A	B	C	D	E	F	G	H	I	J	K
1	Name	Department	Hours Worked	Hourly Pay	Total Pay						Departments
2	Reid			$29.37	$0.00						Production
3	Sharma			$36.67	$0.00						Sales
4	Kotsakis			$36.59	$0.00						Administration
5	Harragon			$29.27	$0.00						
6	Chan			$33.19	$0.00						
7	Langlands			$26.55	$0.00						

Specifying a Maximum Value

1) Select the cell(s) you want to apply validation to (in this example cells C2 to C7).

2) Select the **Data** tab on the Ribbon and from the **Data Tools** group, click on the **Data Validation** button ⊑✓⊑⊘ . The "Data Validation" dialog box will be displayed.

3) Click on the **Settings** tab if necessary, and from the **Allow type** drop-down list, select the type of entry you want to allow (e.g. Whole Number, Decimal, List, Date, Time, Text Length, or Custom). In this example, **Whole Numbers** are allowed.

4) From the **Data** drop-down list, select the criteria that you would like to use (e.g. between, equal to, greater than, less than, etc.). In this example, **between** is used.

5) Specify the **Minimum** and **Maximum** values to permit, as required. Note that these entries can be specific values (e.g. 100), or they can reference the value in a cell (e.g. D5). In this example, the **Minimum** value is **0** and the **Maximum** value is **40**.

6) Click on the **Input Message** tab, and enter a **Title** and **Input message**. These will appear as a tooltip when the cell is selected and guide users on what to enter.

7) Click on the **Error Alert** tab, and ensure the **Show error alert after invalid data is entered** is enabled.

8) Select the **Style** of alert to use from the drop-down list:

Stop – Prevents entry of invalid data.

Warning – Warns but allows invalid data if the user chooses to proceed.

Information – Displays a message but does not restrict entry.

9) Add a **Title** for the error alert and a **Error message** if desired.

10) Click **OK** to apply the validation rule.

Restricting the Entries Allowed

One of the most common uses of Data Validation is creating a drop-down list, which ensures users can only select from a predefined set of options. This makes data entry faster, reduces typing errors, and keeps values consistent – especially useful for things like department names, product codes, or status options.

In the following example, the data validation feature is used to ensure that a valid department is entered in cells B2 to B7.

1) In a blank column, type the list of allowed entries (in this example they have been entered in cells K2 to K4).

2) Select the list and assign it a name by selecting the **Formulas** tab on the Ribbon and selecting the **Define Name** command, then enter a name (e.g. "Dept_List").

3) Select the cell(s) where you want the drop-down list to appear (in this example cells B2 to B7).

4) Select the **Data** tab on the Ribbon and from the **Data Tools** group, click on the **Data Validation** button ⊑⊗ .

5) Click on the **Settings** tab if necessary, and from the **Allow type** drop-down list, select **List**.

6) In the Source box, type the equals sign (=) followed by the range name (e.g. **=Dept_List**)

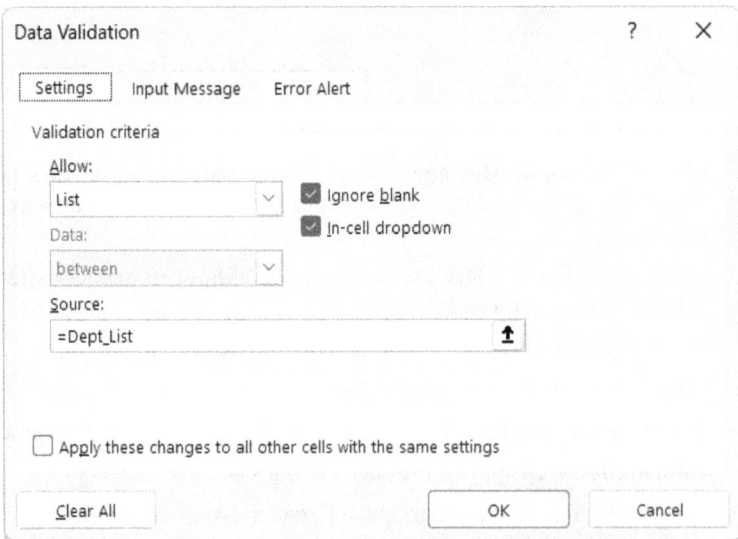

Data Validation		?	✕
Settings Input Message Error Alert			
Validation criteria			
Allow:			
List ∨	☑ Ignore blank		
Data:	☑ In-cell dropdown		
between ∨			
Source:			
=Dept_List ↥			
☐ Apply these changes to all other cells with the same settings			
Clear All		OK	Cancel

7) If desired, complete the information on the **Input Message** and **Error Alert** tabs.

8) Click **OK**. The selected cell(s) contain a drop-down list based on the named range.

Copying Data Validation Rules to Other Cells

After setting up Data Validation rules in Excel (refer to "*Preventing Errors with Data Validation*"), you may find that you want to apply the same rules to another range, or even another workbook. This can be achieved quickly, without having to recreate the rule(s).

1) Select a cell that already has the desired Data Validation rule applied.

2) Press **CTRL+C** (or select the **Home** tab on the Ribbon and click the **Copy** button).

3) Highlight the cell(s) where you want to apply the same rules.

4) Select the **Home** tab on the Ribbon and from the **Clipboard** group, click on the drop-down arrow under the **Paste** button and select the **Paste Special** command. The "Paste Special" dialog box will be displayed.

5) Select the **Validation** option and click **OK**.

This method only copies the Data Validation rules – it does not overwrite cell formatting, contents, or formulas.

Entering Numbers with Decimal Places or Trailing Zeros

Excel can automatically insert decimal places into numbers as you type, or append a fixed number of trailing zeros to large whole numbers. This helps ensure data is entered quickly, consistently, and in the correct format.

1) Select the **File** tab on the Ribbon and then select the **Options** command.

2) Click on **Advanced** from the list of categories on the left of the "Excel Options" dialog box.

3) In the **Editing options** section, enable the **Automatically insert a decimal point** option.

4) In the **Places** box, enter:

A positive number for the number of digits to appear to the right of the decimal point.

A negative number to indicate the number of trailing zeros for large whole numbers.

For example, if you enter 2 in the Places box, typing 98 will display 0.98 and typing 4 will display 0.04. If you enter -3, typing 125 will display 125000.

5) Click **OK** to return to the spreadsheet.

6) When you have finished entering numbers with decimal places or zeros, select the **File** tab on the Ribbon and then select the **Options** command, click the **Advanced** category, and from the **Editing options** section, disable the **Automatically insert a decimal point** option.

When this option is enabled, the message "Fixed Decimal" is displayed in the status bar, as shown below.

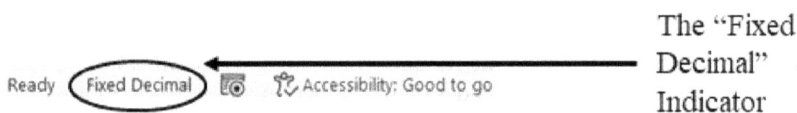

The "Fixed Decimal" Indicator

Ready   Fixed Decimal   Accessibility: Good to go

Note: Data entered before enabling this option is not affected.

Quickly Protecting Cells with Formulas

When you share or update a worksheet, it's often important to prevent accidental changes to formulas while still allowing data entry in other cells. Excel makes this easy by letting you lock only the cells that contain formulas, leaving the rest of the worksheet editable.

The following steps show how to quickly protect formula cells while leaving other cells open, making use of keyboard shortcuts to maximise speed and efficiency.

1) Press **CTRL+A** to select the entire sheet.

2) Press **CTRL+1** to open the "Format Cells" dialog box.

3) On the **Protection** tab, disable the **Locked** check box and click **OK**.

4) Press **F5** to open the "Go To" dialog box and then click the **Special** button. The "Go To Special" dialog box will be displayed.

5) Select the **Formulas** option and click **OK**.

6) Press **CTRL+1**, go to the **Protection** tab, enable the **Locked** option and then click **OK**.

7) Select the **Review** tab on the Ribbon and from the **Protect** group, select the **Protect Sheet** command.

8) Enter a **Password to unprotect sheet** if desired, adjust the protection options if required and then click **OK**.

Cells with formulas will now be protected from editing, while all other cells remain editable.

Note: When the worksheet has been protected, pressing the **TAB** key will move the cell pointer between the unprotected cells, assisting with data entry.

Using Goal Seek to Work Backwards from a Result

The **Goal Seek** feature helps you answer "what-if" questions by working backwards from a desired result. Instead of manually trial-and-error testing different values, Goal Seek automatically adjusts one input to achieve the target outcome.

For example, you might want to know what sales figure is needed to reach a certain profit, or what interest rate would give a specific loan repayment.

1) Select a cell containing a formula that calculates the result you're interested in.

2) Select the **Data** tab and from the **Forecast** group click on the **What-If Analysis** button and then select **Goal Seek**. The "Goal Seek" dialog box will be displayed.

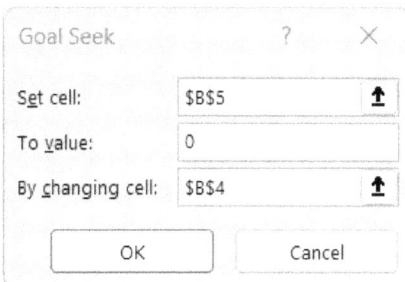

Goal Seek	?	X
Set cell:	$B$5	↑
To value:	0	
By changing cell:	$B$4	↑
OK		Cancel

3) In the **Set cell** field select the cell containing the formula result.

4) In the **To value** field enter the target result you want.

5) In the **By changing cell** field choose the input cell that Excel should adjust.

6) Click **OK**. Excel will test values until it finds a solution.

7) If you're happy with the answer, click **OK** to keep it, otherwise click **Cancel** to return the original value.

Creating Live Pictures of Your Data

Excel's hidden Camera tool allows you to create live snapshots of any cell range and place them elsewhere in your workbook.

The Camera tool is not visible on the Quick Access Toolbar or Ribbon by default, but you can add it from the **All Commands** list (refer to "*Customising the Quick Access Toolbar*" and "*Customising the Ribbon*"). Once added, you'll see the Camera icon on your Quick Access Toolbar or Ribbon.

1) Select the range of cells you want to capture.

2) Click the **Camera** icon.

3) Move to the location where you want the snapshot and click once to place it.

The snapshot behaves like a picture, so you can resize or move it as needed. Best of all, it stays linked to the source data and updates automatically if the original values change. This makes it especially useful for building dashboards that consolidate figures from multiple sheets, or for keeping a live view of sales totals, KPIs, or project milestones on screen.

THE RIBBON AND TOOLBARS

Moving the Quick Access Toolbar

The Quick Access Toolbar is a small, customisable toolbar that gives you one-click access to your most frequently used commands. By default, the Quick Access Toolbar appears above the Ribbon (next to the Excel title bar), however it can also be repositioned to sit underneath the Ribbon, making it closer to your worksheet commands.

1) Click the small drop-down arrow at the end of the Quick Access Toolbar.

Drop-down arrow
at end of the
Quick Access Toolbar

2) From the drop-down menu, select the **Show Below the Ribbon** command.

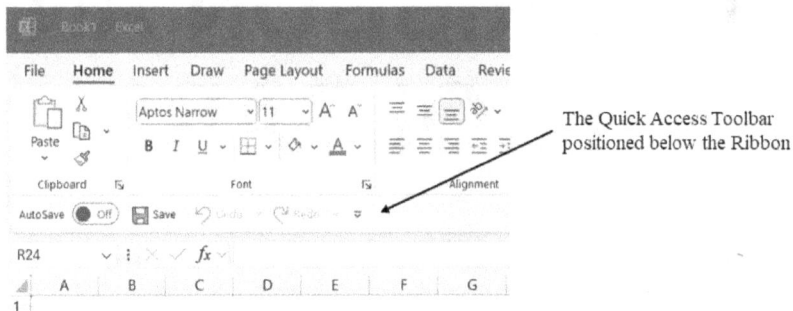

The Quick Access Toolbar positioned below the Ribbon

Note: You can move the Quick Access Toolbar back to its original position by repeating the steps above and selecting the **Show Above the Ribbon** command.

Customising the Quick Access Toolbar

By default the Quick Access Toolbar includes common tools such as Save, Undo, and Redo, but you can easily add any command you use regularly.

1) Click the drop-down arrow at the end of the Quick Access Toolbar.

2) From the list, select any common commands you want to add (e.g. New, Open, Print Preview and Print, etc.).

3) To add other commands, select the **More Commands** option. The "Excel Options" dialog box will be displayed.

4) You can choose any command from the left-hand list and click **Add >>** to move it to your Quick Access Toolbar.

5) From the **Choose commands from** drop-down list, select **All Commands** to see a list of all the commands in Excel that you can add to the Quick Access Toolbar.

6) You can use the up and down pointing arrows on the right of the dialog box to reorder commands on the Quick Access Toolbar.

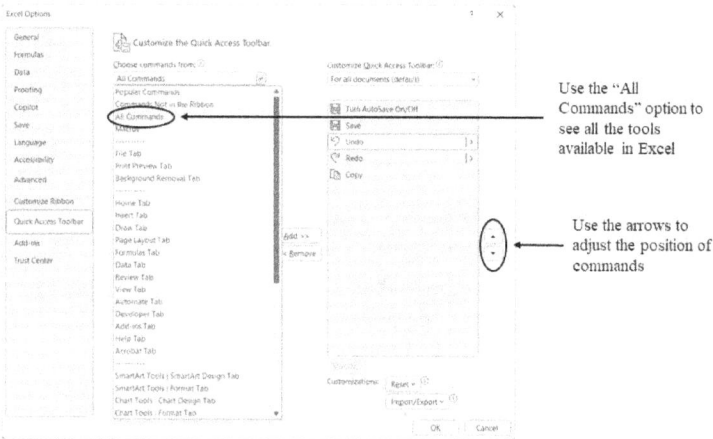

7) Click **OK** to save your changes.

Resetting the Quick Access Toolbar

You can reset the Quick Access Toolbar back to its default state via the following steps:

1) Right-click anywhere on the Quick Access Toolbar.

2) Select **Customize Quick Access Toolbar** from the shortcut menu. The "Excel Options" dialog box will be displayed.

3) In the bottom right of the dialog box, in the **Customizations** section, click the **Reset** button and select **Reset only Quick Access Toolbar** from the drop-down menu.

4) Click **Yes** to confirm, then **OK** to return to the workbook.

Accessing Ribbon Commands via the Keyboard

You can access commands from the Ribbon via the keyboard using the following technique.

1) Press **ALT** (or **F10**). This activates KeyTips. Small letters and numbers will appear over each Ribbon tab and Quick Access Toolbar button.

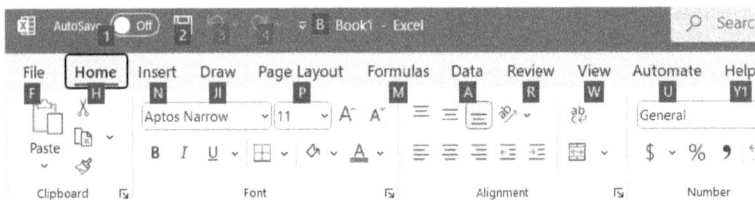

2) Press the key shown for the tab or command you want. For example, press **H** to open the **Home** tab or **N** for the **Insert** tab.

3) Once the tab is open, additional letters and numbers will appear for each command. Continue pressing the keys shown to navigate to your desired command.

4) To execute the command, press **Enter** (if required) to activate the command you've selected.

Note: If you know the full sequence, you can type it without pausing. For example, **Alt H V S** opens the "Paste Special" dialog box.

Collapsing the Ribbon

You can quickly collapse the Ribbon to create more space in your worksheet. Just double-click any Ribbon tab, such as **Home** or **Insert**, and the Ribbon will collapse so that only the tab names are shown. To bring it back, simply double-click a tab again and the full Ribbon will reappear.

This quick toggle is a useful way to maximise your working area without permanently changing any settings.

The Mini Toolbar

The Mini Toolbar is a small, semi-transparent toolbar that appears when you right-click a cell, range, or text. It provides quick access to the most common formatting commands, saving you from having to move your mouse back to the Ribbon.

1)   Select the cell(s) or text you want to format.

2)   Right-click the selection. The mini toolbar will appear just above or just below the shortcut menu.

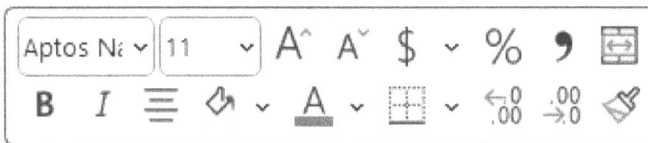

3)   Move the mouse over the Mini Toolbar and click on the desired formatting option.

If you find the mini toolbar distracting, you can disable it completely:

1)   Select the **File** tab on the Ribbon and then select the **Options** command.

2)   Click on the **General** category and in the **User Interface options**, disable **Show Mini Toolbar on selection**.

3)   Click **OK** to return to the workbook.

Customising the Ribbon

You can customise the Ribbon to add, remove, or rearrange commands so that it works in the way you prefer.

1)   Right-click the Ribbon and select the **Customise the Ribbon** command.

The "Excel Options" dialog box is displayed, with two lists displayed – the one on the left showing the available commands in Excel and the one on the right showing the current Ribbon tabs and groups.

Available commands

Current Ribbon configuration

2) From the list on the right, select a Tab and group where you want to add a command.

3) Select a command from the left list and click **Add >>** to place it into the selected tab or group.

4) From the **Choose commands from** drop-down list, select **All Commands** to see a list of all the commands in Excel that you can add to the Ribbon.

5) Use the up and down pointing arrows on the right of the dialog box to rearrange the order of tabs, groups, or commands.

6) Click **OK** to apply your changes.

Note: You can also remove commands or whole groups from the Ribbon by selecting them in the right list and clicking Remove.

Creating New Tabs and Groups on the Ribbon

The Ribbon is designed to make commands easy to find by organising them into tabs (e.g. Home, Insert, Formulas) and further into groups (e.g. Font or Alignment on the Home tab).

While Excel provides many built-in tabs and groups, you can customise the Ribbon to suit your own preferences by creating new tabs and adding groups that contain the commands you use most often. This helps streamline your tasks and ensures frequently used commands are always accessible.

1) Right-click the Ribbon and select **Customise the Ribbon**.

2) Click **New Tab** at the bottom of the right-hand list to create a new custom tab. Excel will create a new tab and a new group inside it.

3) Select the new tab, click **Rename**, enter in a name for the new tab you have created and click **OK**.

4) Select the new group, click **Rename**, enter in a name for the new group and click **OK**.

5) Select a command to add to your custom tab from the left-hand panel, and click **Add >>** to place it into your group.

6) To create a new grouping of commands, with the new custom tab selected, click **New Group**.

7) Select the newly added group, click **Rename**, enter in a name for the new group you have created and click **OK**.

8) Continue adding commands and groups to your new tab as necessary.

9) Use the Up and Down arrows on the right of the dialog box to reorder tabs, groups, or commands if needed. You can also right-click on an item to select the **Remove** command if required.

10) Click **OK** to save your changes. Your new tab will now appear on the Ribbon, ready for use.

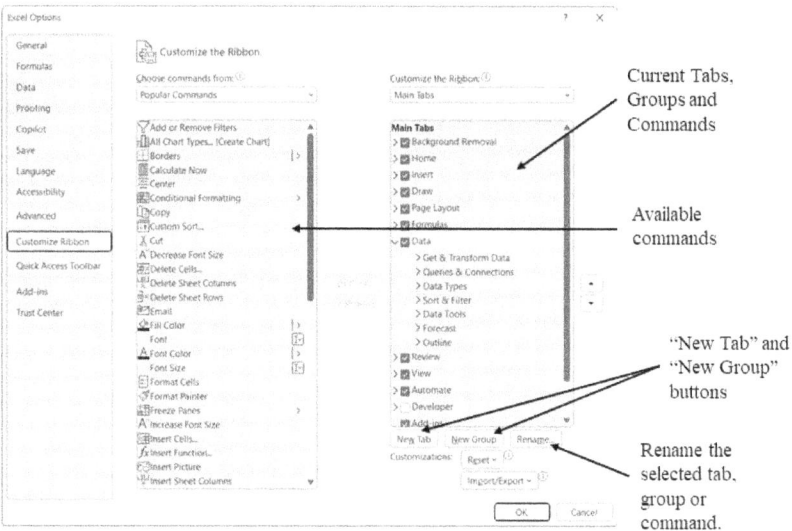

Resetting the Ribbon

You can reset the Ribbon back to its default state via the following steps:

1) Right-click anywhere on the Ribbon.

2) Select **Customize the Ribbon** from the shortcut menu. The "Excel Options" dialog box will be displayed.

3) In the bottom right of the dialog box, in the **Customizations** section, click the **Reset** button and select **Reset only selected Ribbon tab** from the drop-down menu.

4) Click **OK** to return to the workbook.

Note: The **Reset all customizations** option restores both the Ribbon and the Quick Access Toolbar to Excel's default settings.

MACROS

Working with Macros

Macros provide a method of quickly performing repetitive or unusual tasks. A macro is a series of commands that are stored together and can be run whenever you need to perform a certain task.

Macros can either be recorded or written as code in Visual Basic for Applications (VBA). The sample macros in this chapter have all been written in VBA. You can create the macros described in this chapter by completing the following steps and inserting the relevant macro commands (which are displayed in this typeface) at step 5 of the procedure.

1) Ensure that all files have been closed.

2) Select the **View** tab on the Ribbon, then from the **Window** group, click **Unhide**. If **PERSONAL.XLSB** appears in the list, select it and click **OK**. If it does not appear, Excel will create it automatically the first time you record a macro to the Personal Macro Workbook.

3) Press **ALT+F11** to open the "Microsoft Visual Basic for Applications" editor.

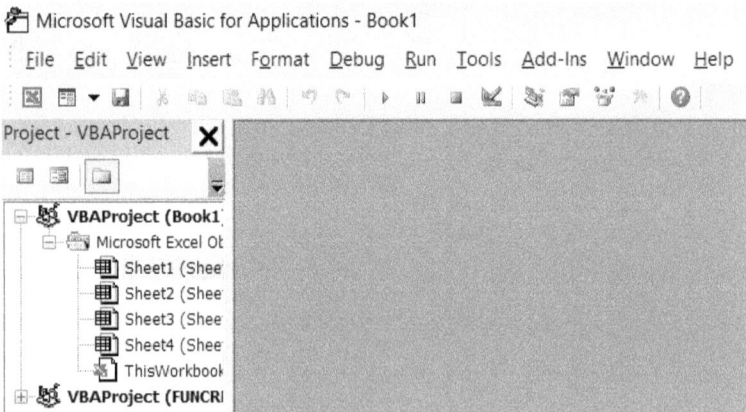

4) From the menu in the VBA Editor, select **Insert ➔ Module** to create a new module.

5) Type or paste the required VBA macro commands into the module (the macros in this book are shown in this typeface).

6)   Close the VBA Editor by clicking the **X** in the top-right corner of the window, or by pressing **ALT+Q**, which will return you to Excel.

7)   On the Ribbon, go to the **View** tab and from the **Window** group, click **Hide**. This will hide the Personal Macro Workbook. When you close Excel, choose **Yes** when prompted to save changes to **PERSONAL.XLSB**, to ensure your macro is stored permanently.

8)   To run a macro go to the **View** tab and in the **Macros** group, click the **Macros** button. The "Macro" dialog box will be displayed. Select the macro that you want to run and click the **Run** button.

Note: Macros can also be run via keyboard shortcuts (refer to "*Assigning a Macro to a Keyboard Shortcut*") or by assigning them to the Quick Access Toolbar (refer to "*Assigning Macros to The Quick Access Toolbar*" or to the Ribbon (refer to "*Assigning Macros to the Ribbon*").

To ensure that a macro can be run in all workbooks it should be stored in the **PERSONAL.XLSB** file. If you do not want a macro to be available in all workbooks, ensure the workbook that you want to store the macro in is open and omit steps 2 and 7 from the above procedure.

If the PERSONAL.XLSB file does not exist (i.e. it does not appear in step 2), you can create it by recording any simple macro and choosing to **Store macro in** the **Personal Macro Workbook**. When you save and close Excel, the PERSONAL.XLSB file will be created automatically in your XLSTART folder.

Macro commands that are indented indicate that the macro code on the indented line should be entered together with the preceding line as one continuous command (line) in Visual Basic for Applications. In the following example, both parts of the macro code should be entered as one continuous line.

```
Set MyRange =
        ActiveSheet.Range(ActiveWindow.Cell.Addr
ess)
```

Assigning a Macro to a Keyboard Shortcut

Excel allows you to assign macros to specific keyboard shortcuts, providing a quick method of running (executing) the macro.

The following steps describe how to assign or change a keyboard shortcut associated with a macro.

1) Go to the **View** tab on the Ribbon and from the **Macros** group, click on the drop-down arrow under the **Macros** button and then select **View Macros**. The "Macro" dialog box will be displayed.
(You can also press **ALT+F8** to open the Macro dialog directly.)

2) Select the macro you want to assign a shortcut key to and click the **Options** button.

3) Type the letter you want to use for your shortcut. By default, the shortcut will be **CTRL+letter**. If you also hold down the **SHIFT** key, the shortcut becomes **CTRL+SHIFT+letter**.

4) Click **OK** to return to the "Macro" dialog box and then click **Cancel** to close the Macro dialog box.

Note: Keyboard shortcuts can either consist of **CTRL** and a letter, or **CTRL+SHIFT** and a letter – this provides a total of 52 possible shortcut key combinations that you can use. If **CAPS LOCK** is on when you assign a keyboard shortcut, Excel will automatically treat it as a **CTRL+SHIFT** combination.

Keyboard shortcuts assigned to macros take precedence over program shortcut keys. For example assigning **CTRL+S** to a macro means that when you press this keyboard combination the macro will run, and its standard function (in this example "Save") will not be available.

Assigning Macros to The Quick Access Toolbar

One of the quickest ways to run a macro is to assign it to a button on the Quick Access Toolbar (refer to "*Customising the Quick Access Toolbar*").

The following steps describe how to add a macro to the Quick Access Toolbar.

1) Click the drop-down arrow at the end of the Quick Access Toolbar and then select **More Commands**.

2) From the **Choose commands from** drop-down list, select **Macros**.

3) Select the macro that you want to add from the left-hand list and click **Add >>** to move it into your Quick Access Toolbar.

4) From the list of commands on the right-hand side of the dialog box, select the macro that you have added to the Quick Access Toolbar and click the **Modify** button. The "Modify Button" dialog box will be displayed.

5) Select a button **Symbol** and if required, adjust the **Display name** for the macro and then click **OK** twice to return to the workbook. The macro will now appear on the Quick Access Toolbar, ready for use.

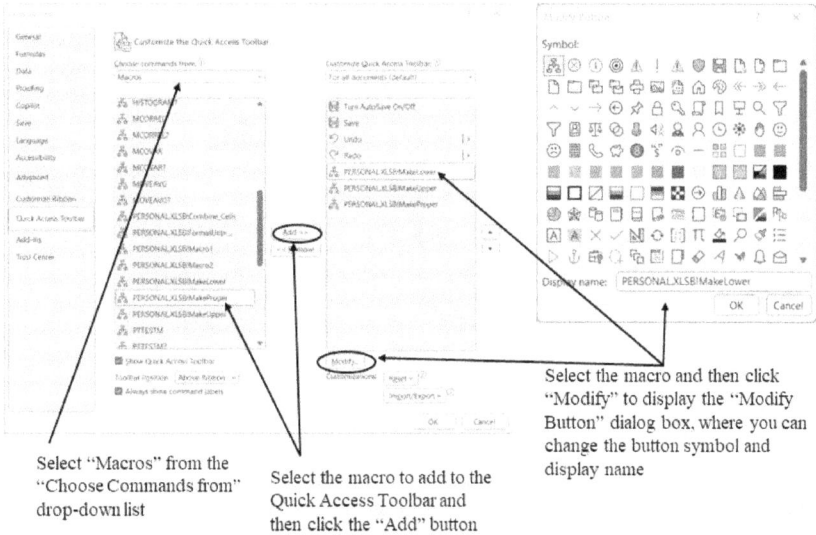

Select "Macros" from the "Choose Commands from" drop-down list

Select the macro to add to the Quick Access Toolbar and then click the "Add" button

Select the macro and then click "Modify" to display the "Modify Button" dialog box, where you can change the button symbol and display name

Assigning Macros to the Ribbon

Another method of running a macro is to add it to one of the tabs on the Ribbon (refer to "*Customising the Ribbon*"). You can add macros to existing tabs, or to custom tabs that you have created (refer to "*Creating New Tabs and Groups on the Ribbon*").

The following steps describe how to add a macro to the Ribbon.

1) Right-click the Ribbon and select **Customize the Ribbon**.

2) From the **Choose commands from** drop-down list, select **Macros**.

3) Select the macro that you want to add from the left-hand list and click **Add >>** to move it into your Quick Access Toolbar.

4) From the list of commands on the right-hand side of the dialog box, select the macro that you have added to the Ribbon and click the **Modify** button. The "Modify Button" dialog box will be displayed.

5) Select a button **Symbol** and if required, adjust the **Display name** for the macro and then click **OK** to return to the "Excel Options" dialog box.

6) Use the Up and Down arrows on the right of the dialog box to position the macro in the desired tab and group.

7) Click **OK** to save your changes. The macro will now appear on the Ribbon, ready for use.

Including a Status Message when a Macro is Running

When running macros that take a while to execute, it can be difficult to tell whether the macro is still processing, has finished, or has stopped responding. For instance, applying the Change Case macros (see "*Changing Case Macros*") to several thousand cells may take a few minutes to complete.

You can add the following line of code at the start of the macro (just after the "Sub" line) so that a message will be displayed on the status bar (at the bottom of the screen) as the macro runs.

```
Application.StatusBar="Macro Executing. Please
Wait..."
```

Include the following line of code at the end of the macro (just before the "End Sub" line) to ensure that the message on the status bar is removed.

```
Application.StatusBar=False
```

Preventing Screen Updates when a Macro is Running

Macros that perform many actions, such as selecting cells, entering values or formulas, or forcing recalculations, can cause the screen to flicker as Excel redraws each step. This slows execution and can also be visually distracting. To improve performance and run the macro more smoothly, add the following line at the beginning of your code.

```
Application.ScreenUpdating = False
```

You should restore the screen updating when the macro finishes, via the following line of code inserted at the end of your macro.

```
Application.ScreenUpdating = True
```

Display Filename and Pathname in Title Bar

The following macro displays the full path and filename of the currently opened file in the Title Bar. The macro needs to be run for each file opened or if the current file is renamed using the "Save As" command.

```
Sub ChangeCaption()
ActiveWindow.Caption = ActiveWorkbook.FullName
End Sub
```

Removing Hyperlinks from the Selected Range

Sometimes spreadsheets end up filled with unwanted hyperlinks, for example, when data is copied from the web or email addresses are auto-formatted. This macro removes hyperlinks (and their blue/underlined formatting) but leaves the actual text in place.

To use it, select the range of cells you want to clean up and then run the macro.

```
Sub DeleteHyperSelection()
Selection.Hyperlinks.Delete
End Sub
```

Note: The macro will remove all formatting applied to the cell(s) containing hyperlinks.

Changing Case Macros

You can use worksheet functions to change the case of text (refer to *"Converting the Case of Text"*), however if you have to repeat this function often, you may want to create macros that perform these tasks for you.

Ensure that you have selected the range of cells that you want to change the case of before running any of these macros.

Uppercase Macro

```
Sub MakeUpper()
Dim c As Range
For Each c In Selection
If VarType(c.Value) = vbString Then c.Value =
      UCase(c.Value)
Next
End Sub
```

Lowercase Macro

```
Sub MakeLower()
Dim c As Range
For Each c In Selection
If VarType(c.Value) = vbString Then c.Value =
      LCase(c.Value)
Next
End Sub
```

Proper Case Macro

```
Sub MakeProper()
Dim c As Range
For Each c In Selection
If VarType(c.Value) = vbString Then c.Value =
      Application.WorksheetFunction.Proper(c.Value)
Next
End Sub
```

Combining Cell Contents Macro

There may be times when you need to join the contents of several cells together. This can be done via the TEXTJOIN function (refer to "*Joining Cells Together*"), however if you have to repeat this function often, you may want to create a macro to perform the task for you.

The following macro will combine the contents of the selected cells (on each row), into the one cell entry (in the first column of the selection). The original data in the individual cells is deleted, so that only the combined data (joined together in one cell) is displayed.

Ensure that you select the range containing the cells that you want to join together before running the macro.

```
Sub Combine_Cells()
Dim r As Range, c As Range, s As String
For Each r In Selection.Rows
s = ""
For Each c In r.Cells
If c.Value <> "" Then s = s & IIf(Len(s) > 0, " ",
    "") & c.Value
c.ClearContents
Next c
r.Cells(1).Value = s
Next r
End Sub
```

Displaying Unprotected Cells in Blue

When using Excel's protection feature, it is often difficult to detect which cells are protected and which cells are unprotected (ie: are able to have data entered in them). The following macro checks the protection status of the currently selected cells. Unprotected cells containing data display with blue text.

Before running the macro, select the range of cells that you want to check. To select the entire populated area of the current worksheet, press **CTRL+HOME** to move to cell A1, then press **SHIFT+CTRL+END**.

```
Sub FormatUnprotected()
Dim cell As Range
For Each cell In Selection
If Not cell.Locked Then
cell.Font.Color = vbBlue
End If
Next cell
End Sub
```

After running the macro, enable Worksheet Protection, so that data can only be entered or edited in the unlocked cells (which will now display in blue).

1) Select the **Review** tab and from the **Protect** group, select the **Protect Sheet** command.

2) If desired, enter a **Password to unprotect sheet** and then click **OK**.

Print Each Group on a Separate Page

When you want each group of records (such as department, client, project, or year) printed on its own page, this macro automatically inserts page breaks for you. It runs on the active sheet in the current workbook.

Before running the macro, sort by your grouping column, then select the full block of cells in that column that covers every record you want grouped – begin at the first data row (exclude the header) and finish at the last data row.

The macro removes any existing manual page breaks, then adds a horizontal page break before each row where the key value changes from the row above. The result is a clean printout with neatly divided sections, ready for distribution.

```
Sub PageBreakOnChange()
Dim rng As Range, i As Long, r As Long
If TypeName(Selection) <> "Range" Then Exit Sub
Set rng = Selection.Columns(1)
If rng.Rows.Count < 2 Then Exit Sub
Application.ScreenUpdating = False
With ActiveWorkbook.ActiveSheet
.DisplayPageBreaks = False
.ResetAllPageBreaks
For i = 2 To rng.Rows.Count
r = rng.Cells(i, 1).Row
If rng.Cells(i, 1).Value <> rng.Cells(i - 1,
        1).Value Then
.HPageBreaks.Add Before:=.Rows(r)
End If
Next i
.DisplayPageBreaks = True
End With
Application.ScreenUpdating = True
End Sub
```

Generate Random Numbers Without Duplicates

This macro fills any selected cells (including non-contiguous ranges) with unique random integers between a user-specified lower and upper value. Every number is guaranteed to be unique and no duplicates will appear, provided you don't select more cells than the number of available integers.

```
Sub FillRandomNoDups()
Dim x As Variant, lo As Long, hi As Long, need As
        Long
Dim v As Variant, i As Long, j As Long, k As Long,
        t As Variant
Dim a As Range, c As Range
If TypeName(Selection) <> "Range" Then Exit Sub
x = Application.InputBox("Lowest Possible Number:",
        Type:=1): If x = False Then Exit Sub Else lo =
        CLng(x)
x = Application.InputBox("Highest Possible Number",
        Type:=1): If x = False Then Exit Sub Else hi =
        CLng(x)
If hi < lo Then MsgBox "Highest Possible Number must
        be greater than the Lowest Possible Number":
        Exit Sub
need = CLng(Selection.CountLarge)
If need > hi - lo + 1 Then
MsgBox "Not enough unique integers in the specified
        range."
Exit Sub
End If
v = Evaluate("ROW(" & lo & ":" & hi & ")")
Randomize
For i = UBound(v, 1) To 2 Step -1
j = Int(Rnd * i) + 1
t = v(i, 1): v(i, 1) = v(j, 1): v(j, 1) = t
Next i
k = 1
For Each a In Selection.Areas
For Each c In a.Cells
c.Value = v(k, 1)
k = k + 1
If k > need Then Exit Sub
Next c
Next a
End Sub
```

Converting Formula Results to Values Macro

The **Paste Special** (**Values**) command can be very useful for converting the results of formulas back to values (refer to "*Pasting Values Instead of Formulas*").

If you regularly perform this function, the following macro can be used to automate the process. Ensure that the cells you want to convert to values are selected before running the macro.

```
Sub ReplaceWithValues()
Selection.Value = Selection.Value
End Sub
```

Deleting All Named Ranges

Named ranges in Excel can be incredibly useful, but over time, they often pile up, become outdated, or break due to changes in the workbook. This clutter can slow down performance, cause formula errors, and make auditing more difficult. The following macro will delete all range names from a workbook.

Note: Deleting names will affect anything that references them. This includes formulas, charts, data validation rules, conditional formatting, print areas and print titles, and any VBA code that uses those names.

```
Sub DeleteAllNamedRangesFromActiveWorkbook()
Dim nm As Name
Dim countDeleted As Long
countDeleted = 0
For Each nm In ActiveWorkbook.Names
On Error Resume Next
nm.Delete
If Err.Number = 0 Then countDeleted = countDeleted +
      1
On Error GoTo 0
Next nm
MsgBox countDeleted & " named ranges deleted from
      active workbook.", vbInformation, "Range Names
      Deleted"
End Sub
```

Conditionally Coloured Charts

This macro automatically colours the data points in a chart based on whether they are above or below a user-defined threshold. When the macro runs, it prompts you to enter a cut-off value. It then loops through every series in the active chart and applies conditional formatting: values greater than or equal to the threshold are displayed in blue, and values below are highlighted in red.

Ensure that you have selected a chart (e.g. a bar chart or column chart) before running the macro.

```
Sub ConditionalColorChart()
Dim chrt As Chart, ser As Series, vals As Variant
Dim i As Long, THRESH As Double, userInput As
      Variant
userInput = Application.InputBox("Enter the
      threshold value:", "Conditional Colour",
      Type:=1)
If userInput = False Then Exit Sub
THRESH = CDbl(userInput)
On Error Resume Next
Set chrt = ActiveChart
If chrt Is Nothing Then Set chrt =
      ActiveSheet.ChartObjects(1).Chart
On Error GoTo 0
If chrt Is Nothing Then Exit Sub
For Each ser In chrt.SeriesCollection
vals = ser.Values
If IsArray(vals) Then
For i = LBound(vals) To UBound(vals)
If IsNumeric(vals(i)) Then
If vals(i) > THRESH Then
ser.Points(i).Format.Fill.ForeColor.RGB = RGB(0,
      112, 192) 'Blue
Else
ser.Points(i).Format.Fill.ForeColor.RGB = RGB(255,
      0, 0) 'Red
End If
End If
Next i
End If
Next ser
End Sub
```

Zooming With the Keyboard

In Excel, most commands can be carried out with either the mouse or the keyboard. However, not every feature is equally accessible. Zooming is a good example – it's simple with the mouse, but there's no quick keyboard shortcut to zoom in or out. To make zooming just as easy from the keyboard, you can create two simple macros and assign them to key combinations.

The MyZoomIn macro increases the zoom level of the active worksheet by 10% at a time, up to Excel's maximum of 400%.

```
Sub MyZoomIn()
If ActiveWindow Is Nothing Then Exit Sub
Dim ZP As Long
ZP = CLng(Int(ActiveWindow.Zoom * 1.1))
If ZP > 400 Then ZP = 400
ActiveWindow.Zoom = ZP
End Sub
```

The MyZoomOut macro decreases the zoom level by 10% at a time, down to Excel's minimum of 10%.

```
Sub MyZoomOut()
If ActiveWindow Is Nothing Then Exit Sub
Dim ZP As Long
ZP = CLng(Int(ActiveWindow.Zoom * 0.9))
If ZP < 10 Then ZP = 10
ActiveWindow.Zoom = ZP
End Sub
```

To get the most from the macros, assign them to keyboard shortcuts (refer to "*Assigning a Macro to a Keyboard Shortcut*").

Listing Worksheet Names Macro

When you have a number of worksheets in a workbook, it is useful to be able to retrieve the worksheet names and put them on their own worksheet, which can be used in a table of contents, for example.

The following macro creates a new worksheet at the end of the active workbook and fills column A with the names of all the worksheets in that workbook, in the same order as the sheet tabs. It then activates the new sheet so the list is visible.

```
Sub GetAllTabNames()
Dim i As Long, sht As Object, toc As Worksheet
Set toc =
      Worksheets.Add(After:=Sheets(Sheets.Count))
On Error Resume Next: toc.Name = "All Tabs": On
      Error GoTo 0
i = 1
For Each sht In Sheets
```

```
If sht.Name <> toc.Name Then
toc.Cells(i, 1).Value = sht.Name
i = i + 1
End If
Next sht
toc.Columns(1).AutoFit
End Sub
```

Sorting Worksheet Tabs Macro

If you have workbooks that contain multiple sheets that you have named (eg: product names, branch names, etc.) you will find the following macro useful – it sorts the worksheet tabs alphabetically.

```
Sub SortSheets()
Dim i As Long, j As Long
For i = 1 To Sheets.Count - 1
For j = i + 1 To Sheets.Count
If UCase(Sheets(j).Name) < UCase(Sheets(i).Name)
Then
Sheets(j).Move Before:=Sheets(i)
End If
Next j
Next i
End Sub
```

Save Each Sheet as its Own Workbook

This macro takes the currently active workbook, checks that it has been saved, and then exports each visible worksheet as its own individual .xlsx file into a folder that you select.

It automatically sanitises worksheet names so they are valid filenames, prevents overwriting by appending a number if a file already exists, and closes each new workbook after saving, while keeping the original workbook open.

At the end, it displays a message confirming that all sheets have been saved separately.

```
Sub SaveSheetsFromActiveWorkbook()
Dim src As Workbook, ws As Worksheet, nb As Workbook
Dim p As String, n As String, f As String, i As
    Long, c As Variant
```

```
Set src = ActiveWorkbook
If src.Path = "" Then MsgBox "Please save this
      workbook first.", vbExclamation, "Save
      Required": Exit Sub
With
      Application.FileDialog(msoFileDialogFolderPick
      er)
.Title = "Select folder": If .Show <> -1 Then Exit
      Sub
p = .SelectedItems(1)
End With
If Right$(p, 1) <> Application.PathSeparator Then p
      = p & Application.PathSeparator
Application.ScreenUpdating = False:
      Application.DisplayAlerts = False
On Error GoTo CleanUp
For Each ws In src.Worksheets
If ws.Visible = xlSheetVisible Then
ws.Copy: Set nb = ActiveWorkbook
n = Trim$(ws.Name): If n = "" Then n = "Sheet"
For Each c In Array("<", ">", ":", """", "/", "\",
      "|", "?", "*"): n = Replace$(n, c, "_"): Next
f = p & n & ".xlsx": i = 1
Do While Len(Dir$(f)) > 0: i = i + 1: f = p & n & "
      (" & i & ").xlsx": Loop
nb.SaveAs Filename:=f, FileFormat:=xlOpenXMLWorkbook
nb.Close False
End If
Next ws
CleanUp:
Application.DisplayAlerts = True:
      Application.ScreenUpdating = True
If Not src Is Nothing Then src.Activate
If Err.Number <> 0 Then
MsgBox "Error: " & Err.Description, vbExclamation
Else
MsgBox "Finished. Each sheet has been saved as a
      separate worksheet.", vbInformation, "Save
      Sheets"
End If
End Sub
```

KEYBOARD SHORTCUTS

Key	Function
ALT+; (semi colon)	Selects only the visible cells (ie: not the hidden cells) in a highlighted range containing hidden columns and rows.
ALT+' (single quote)	Displays the "Style" dialog box.
ALT+= (equal sign)	AutoSum.
ALT+down arrow	Displays a list of existing text entries in a column, allowing you to quickly select one of these values to enter in the current cell.
ALT+ENTER	Starts a new line in the current cell. Used to create multiple line cells for headings.
ALT+F1	Creates a chart embedded in the current sheet.
ALT+F11	Displays the Visual Basic for Applications (VBA) Editor.
ALT+F2 F12	Displays the "Save As" dialog box.
ALT+F4	Exits the current session of Excel.
ALT+F8	Displays the "Macro" dialog box, where macros can be run, edited or deleted.
ALT+PGDN	Moves one screen to the right.
ALT+PGUP	Moves one screen to the left.
ALT+SHIFT+F1 SHIFT+F11	Creates a new worksheet within the current Excel file.
ALT+SHIFT+F2 SHIFT+F12 CTRL+S	Saves the current spreadsheet.
ALT+SHIFT+left arrow	Ungroups selected rows or columns.

Key	Function
ALT+SHIFT+right arrow	Groups together selected rows or columns.
ALT+spacebar	Opens the Excel window control menu (minimise, maximise, close).
CTRL+. (full stop)	Moves to the next corner of the selected area.
CTRL+/	Selects the entire array formula range if the cell pointer is in an array
CTRL+; (semi colon)	Inserts the date into the active cell.
CTRL+[	Selects cells that are directly referred to by the formula in the currently selected cell(s).
CTRL+]	Selects cells containing formulas that make direct use of the value in the currently selected cell(s).
CTRL+` (the key with the ~)	Alternates between displaying formula results (values) and the formulas themselves in cells.
CTRL+' (single quote)	Copies the value from the cell directly above the active cell. If the cell above the active cell contains a formula, the formula is duplicated (with no adjustments for relative positioning).
CTRL+0 (zero)	Hides the selected columns.
CTRL+1	Displays the "Format Cells" dialog box.
CTRL+5	Applies/removes strikethrough formatting.
CTRL+6	Alternates between displaying drawing objects (including charts), showing placeholders for objects (charts only), and hiding drawing objects (including charts).
CTRL+8	Alternates between displaying and hiding outline symbols when data has been grouped.

Key	Function
CTRL+9	Hides the selected rows.
CTRL+A	First press: Selects the current region (contiguous data). Second press: Selects the entire worksheet. In a function argument: Opens the Insert Function dialog.
CTRL+ALT+left arrow	When multiple ranges are selected, moves to the left between the selections.
CTRL+ALT+right arrow	When multiple ranges are selected, moves to the right between the selections.
CTRL+ALT+V	Displays the "Paste Special" dialog box.
CTRL+B CTRL+2	Applies/removes bold formatting.
CTRL+C	Copies the selected cells.
CTRL+D	Fills the active cell with the contents of the cell above. If a range of cells is selected, the value from the first cell in the range is copied to the selected cells underneath it. If the cell being duplicated contains a formula, the formula is copied and adjusted for relative referencing.
CTRL+END	Moves to the last cell of the worksheet (Excel defines this as the intersecting cell from the right-most used column and the bottom-most used row).
CTRL+ENTER	Fills the selected cells with the data or formula entered in the active cell.
CTRL+F10	Maximises the active window if it is not already maximised, otherwise restores the active window.

Key	Function
CTRL+F12 CTRL+ALT+F2 CTRL+O	Displays the "Open" dialog box.
CTRL+F1	Toggles the display of the Ribbon on/off.
CTRL+F3	Displays the "Name Manager" dialog box.
CTRL+F4 CTRL+W	Closes the active workbook.
CTRL+F5	Restores the active window if maximised.
CTRL+F6 CTRL+TAB	When more than one workbook is open, moves forward through the open workbooks.
CTRL+F7	When the active window is not maximised, allows the window to be moved using the arrow keys on the keyboard.
CTRL+F8	When the active window is not maximised, allows the window to be sized using the arrow keys on the keyboard.
CTRL+F9	Minimises the active window.
CTRL+H	Displays the "Find and Replace" dialog box with the "Replace" tab active.
CTRL+HOME	Moves to the beginning of the worksheet (cell A1).
CTRL+I CTRL+3	Applies/removes italic formatting.
CTRL+K	Displays the "Insert Hyperlink" dialog box.
CTRL+minus sign	Deletes the selected row(s) or column(s). If there are no currently selected rows or columns, the "Delete" dialog box is displayed.

Key	Function
CTRL+N	Creates a new Excel workbook.
CTRL+PGDN	Moves to the next sheet in the workbook.
CTRL+PGUP	Moves to the previous sheet in the workbook.
CTRL+R	Fills the active cell with the contents of the cell to its left. If a range of cells is selected, the value from the first cell in the range is copied to the selected cells to its right. If the cell being duplicated contains a formula, the formula is copied and adjusted for relative referencing.
CTRL+SHIFT+; (semi colon)	Inserts the time into the active cell.
CTRL+SHIFT+[	Selects all precedent cells (cells referred to directly or indirectly in the active cell's formula).
CTRL+SHIFT+]	Selects all dependent cells (cells with formulas that reference the active cell).
CTRL+SHIFT+_	Removes all borders from the selected cell(s).
CTRL+SHIFT+` (the key with the ~)	Applies the "General" number format.
CTRL+SHIFT+' (single quote)	Copies the value from the cell directly above the active cell. If the cell above the active cell contains a formula, the result of the formula (not the formula itself) is copied into the cell.
CTRL+SHIFT+= (equal sign)	Inserts row(s) at the selected row(s), or column(s) at the selected column(s). If there are no currently selected rows or columns, the "Insert" dialog box is displayed.

Key	Function
CTRL+SHIFT+1	Applies the "Number" format, with 2 decimal places, thousands separator and negative numbers preceded with a minus symbol (-).
CTRL+SHIFT+2	Applies the "Time" format (12 hour, AM/PM format).
CTRL+SHIFT+3	Applies the "Date" format (d-mm-yy).
CTRL+SHIFT+4	Applies the "Currency" number format, with 2 decimal places and negative numbers in brackets.
CTRL+SHIFT+5	Applies the "Percentage" format, with no decimal places.
CTRL+SHIFT+6	Applies the "Scientific/Exponential" format, with 2 decimal places.
CTRL+SHIFT+7	Applies a single, outline border around the selected cells.
CTRL+SHIFT+8	Selects the region around the active cell (this is the area bounded by blank columns and blank rows).
CTRL+SHIFT+9	Unhides rows between the selected rows.
CTRL+SHIFT+A	Inserts the names of a function's arguments (provided a valid function name has been entered).
CTRL+SHIFT+arrow key	Selects cells in the direction of the arrow key until a blank cell is reached.
CTRL+SHIFT+END	Selects cells to the last active cell on the worksheet.
CTRL+SHIFT+F12 CTRL+P	Displays the "Print" dialog box.

Key	Function
CTRL+SHIFT+F3	Displays the "Create Names from Selection" dialog box (to define names based on row/column labels).
CTRL+SHIFT+F6 CTRL+SHIFT+TAB	When more than one spreadsheet is open, moves backwards through the open spreadsheets.
CTRL+SHIFT+L	Toggles AutoFilter on/off.
CTRL+SHIFT+O (letter O)	Selects all cells containing comments/notes.
CTRL+SHIFT+U	Expand/collapse the formula bar.
CTRL+SHIFT+spacebar	When a cell is selected, selects all cells on the current worksheet. When a drawing object or chart is selected, selects all the objects on the current worksheet.
CTRL+spacebar	Selects the entire column.
CTRL+Q	Displays the Quick Analysis Tool.
CTRL+U CTRL+4	Applies/removes underline formatting.
CTRL+V	Pastes the contents of the clipboard.
CTRL+X	Cuts the selected content.
CTRL+Z	Reverses the last action (Undo).
F1	Displays "Help" in the right pane.
F10 ALT	Activates the Ribbon KeyTips (keyboard shortcuts for Ribbon commands).
F2	Edits the contents of the active cell.
F3	Displays the "Paste Names" dialog box.

Key	Function
F4 CTRL+Y	Repeats the last command/action. When creating a formula, the F4 key cycles the current cell reference between absolute and relative referencing.
F5 CTRL+G	Displays the "Go To" dialog box.
F6	Moves focus between worksheet, Ribbon, task pane, status bar, etc. When the window is split, moves forward through the different areas of the split screen.
F7	Displays the "Spelling" dialog box.
F8	Turns the "extend" feature on and off. This feature allows you to select cells with the arrow keys on the keyboard.
F9	Recalculates all formulas in all open workbooks.
F11	Generates a chart on a new sheet.
HOME	Moves to the beginning of the current row (column A).
PGDN	Moves down one screen.
PGUP	Moves up one screen.
SHIFT+backspace	When multiple cells are selected, cancels the selection and returns the cell pointer to the active cell.
SHIFT+F10	Activates the shortcut menu (equivalent to right-clicking in a cell).
SHIFT+F2	Creates or edits a cell Note.
SHIFT+F3	Displays the "Insert Function" dialog box.

Key	Function
SHIFT+F4	Repeats the last find operation.
SHIFT+F5 CTRL+F	Displays the "Find" dialog box.
SHIFT+F6	Moves focus backwards between panes / Ribbon / task panes. When the window is split, moves backwards through the different areas of the split screen.
SHIFT+F8	Adds to a range selected with the F8 (Extend) feature. For example, press F8, select a series of cells, press SHIFT+F8, move the cell pointer to a new location and then use F8 to select a separate group of cells.
SHIFT+F9	Recalculates formulas on the active sheet only.
SHIFT+spacebar	Selects the entire row.

www.ingramcontent.com/pod-product-compliance
Lightning Source LLC
Chambersburg PA
CBHW060546200326
41521CB00007B/509